Garuda and the Serpents

Garuda and the Serpents

Stories of Friends and Foes from Hindu Mythology

Arshia Sattar

Illustrated by

Ishan Trivedi

JUGGERNAUT BOOKS
KS House, 118 Shahpur Jat, New Delhi 110049, India

First published by Juggernaut Books 2018

10 9 8 7 6 5 4 3 2 1

ISBN 9789386228710

Typeset in Adobe Caslon Pro by R. Ajith Kumar, Noida

Printed at Thomson Press India Ltd.

Contents

1. The Churning of the Ocean 1
2. Garuda and the Serpents 11
3. Bhagiratha Brings Ganga to the Earth 23
4. The Magic Cow 33
5. Takshaka's Revenge 45
6. Shukra and Kacha 57
7. Jambavan, King of the Bears 69
8. Vali and Sugriva 79
9. The Death of Vali 91
10. Hanuman Leaps for the Sun 103
11. Hanuman's Adventures 113
12. When Bhima Met His Brother 133
13. Vritra Swallows Indra 145

14. The Cursed Immortal 155

15. Trishanku's Heaven 167

16. Prahlada and the Magic Cloak 177

17. The Wondrous Story of King Ila 187

18. Mahishasura and the Goddess 197

Note on the Author 207

Note on the Illustrator 208

1

The Churning of the Ocean

One day, the sage Durvasas, who is known for his bad temper, saw Indra, king of the gods, going by on an elephant. As it happened, Durvasas was in a mellow mood and he gave Indra a garland of beautiful flowers. Indra did not think much of it and hung the garland around the neck of the elephant he was riding. The elephant was uncomfortable. He pulled off the garland with his trunk and tossed it to the ground. Then, he stepped on it, trampling it into the dust. Durvasas was enraged – he could not believe that Indra had shown so little respect for the gift he had been given. He cursed the king of the gods to lose all his physical strength, his power, his glory, even his kingdom.

Indra realized his mistake and tried to make amends. But Durvasas was not to be pacified and went off in a great huff. Soon enough, the gods began to lose their battles with the asuras and before long Bali, the asura king, was sitting on the throne of heaven. The gods turned to Indra and blamed him for what had happened, but the king of the gods could not think of a way to win his kingdom back. Indra went to Vishnu and begged him for help. 'I must have my kingdom back. The gods cannot live anywhere but in heaven. Help us, Vishnu!' he cried.

Vishnu understood that the only way the gods would once again be superior to the asuras was by drinking amrita, the nectar of immortality. And to get that, they would have to churn the mighty ocean. Mount Mandara would be the churning pole and Vasuki, the divine serpent who was wrapped around the throat of Shiva, would be the churning rope. But the rope would have to be pulled from both ends. Vishnu explained to Indra that the asuras would have to be part of this enterprise: that they would pull one end of the rope and the gods would pull the other. Between them, the ocean would be churned and it would throw up all kinds of marvellous things, including the nectar of immortality. Indra was not at all pleased about making a partnership with the asuras, but if he wanted his kingdom back, he would have to acquire the precious nectar. And he could not do that without including the asuras in his plan.

Indra went to Bali and said, 'Bali, lord of the asuras, we are going to churn the ocean. All kinds of wonderful things will emerge from the ocean when we do this. But we need the asuras to help pull the churning rope from one end. Will you join us?' Bali eagerly agreed, confident that the asuras would have an equal share in whatever gifts the bounteous ocean produced.

The gods and the asuras assembled on a bright and beautiful day. They were all excited and they shouted and laughed and clapped each other on the back. Mount Mandara was brought in as the pole. Smooth as silk, Vasuki slithered off Shiva's neck and wound himself around the mountain, his head on one side and his tail on the other. The asuras rushed to the side of his head and before

the gods could even react they shouted, 'We are taking this side! You hold his tail!' The asuras and the gods grabbed Vasuki's head and tail and started to pull. Mount Mandara began to turn, slowly, slowly, slowly. But equally slowly, it began to sink.

Again, the gods appealed to Vishnu for help. 'How can we churn the ocean if our churning pole is sinking?' they shouted. 'Vishnu, do something!' In a trice, Vishnu turned himself into a giant turtle. He swam to the bottom of the ocean where he slipped under the mountain, holding it firmly on his back. At once, the churning pole steadied and again the gods and the asuras pulled this way and that. They agitated the ocean whose waves rose higher and higher until they seemed to touch the sky. The waters roared and thundered and the gods and the asuras were drenched in salty spray. But they didn't care.

At last, the ocean began to throw up its treasures. Fourteen jewels, bigger and brighter than you have ever seen, spilled forth. Among them was the spectacular Kaustubha, a jewel so magnificent that it could only be worn by Vishnu. As the asuras coughed and sputtered and reeled under the hot breath and poisonous fumes that came out of Vasuki's mouth, the ocean continued to produce wonder after wonder. Along with ninety-nine other horses that were as swift as the wind, Ucchaihshravas, the whitest of white horses, came forth. This was the horse that the sisters Vinata and Kadru would argue over many years later.* Kamadhenu, the cow who could grant every wish, also came out of the ocean,† as did Kalpavriksha, the wishing tree. Another divine tree, the sweet-smelling Parijata, emerged and went to Nandana, Indra's garden. A long time later, Krishna stole the tree and brought it to earth to make his wives happy. But there was still more in store for Indra, king of the gods. The mighty Airavata, best of all the elephants in the three worlds, came out of the roaring waters and became Indra's mount.

A sweetly curved crescent moon rose out of the waves and settled in Shiva's hair. Pearls of immeasurable beauty, softly lustrous, came forth and so did Lakshmi, goddess of wealth. Nidra, goddess of sleep, appeared as well. She was the

---

* See the story of Garuda on page 11.

† See the story of Kamadhenu on page 33.

colour of night, and she was lazy. The apsaras emerged, each more lovely than the one before – Menaka and Urvashi and Punjikasthala and so many others. They became dancers in Indra's court, turning it into a place of pleasure and beauty. Some say that Vishnu's imperishable weapon, the Sudarshana Chakra, came out of the waters along with the pure white shining conch shell that he always carries.

After one thousand years of churning and churning, the great serpent Vasuki vomited, spewing the deadly Halahala poison from his mouth. It was a black oozing mess and so some people call it Kalakuta. At once, the gods and the asuras were in disarray, they ran hither and thither, knowing that nothing in the world could counter Halahala. Shiva was watching the commotion from far away and he knew that only he could help. He came down from his mountain and offered to swallow the poison. He drank it quickly – his eyes turned red, his cheeks bulged, sweat poured from his forehead, his head snapped backwards. Shiva's wife, Parvati, feared for her husband's life and she clasped her hands around his throat, stopping the poison from entering the rest of his body. Shiva recovered but the power of the poison stained his throat forever blue.

At long last, Dhanvantari (who was to become the gods' healer), stepped out of the waters, holding a pot. In it was amrita, the nectar of immortality, the miraculous potion that could defeat Death, the drink that everyone had been waiting for. The gods and the asuras dropped Vasuki and ran towards Dhanvantari and the pot. The asuras got there first and made off with the precious pot. The gods became very agitated and wailed and beat their breasts. As usual, they went running to Vishnu and threw themselves at his feet. 'The nectar of immortality, that amrita, was supposed to be for us. Now the asuras have it! What shall we do?' they cried together.

Before their astonished eyes, Vishnu transformed himself into Mohini, a woman even more beautiful and alluring than the apsaras that had emerged from the ocean. Mohini's waist was slim and supple, her eyes were like lotus petals, her skin gleamed like soft moonlight, her lips were the colour of forest berries, and when she smiled, it was as if the three worlds held their breath. Mohini swayed over to where the asuras were and distracted them. They were enchanted by her, and in their eagerness to get her attention, they dropped the pot of amrita and chased after her. Immediately, the gods swooped down and made off with the pot. Gleefully, they began to drink from it, convinced that now they would always have the upper hand against all their enemies.

But an asura named Svarabhanu disguised himself as a god and slipped in among them. As he drank his share of the amrita, he was noticed by the Sun and the Moon, who recognized him for who he truly was. They quickly alerted Mohini and she threw Vishnu's discus at the asura, slicing off his head. Since the amrita was still in his mouth, his head became immortal and he came to be known as Rahu. Now Rahu is the asura of the eclipse and all year long he chases the Sun and the Moon across the skies seeking revenge for what they did to him. Every now and then, Rahu catches up with them. He swallows them and holds them in his mouth, but just for a little while, for the Sun and the Moon are protected by the gods.

2

Garuda and the Serpents

The sage Kashyapa had two wives, Vinata and Kadru. They were sisters, but did not always get along. Sometimes they fought over which of them their husband loved more. But the sage left these quarrels alone and offered both the sisters a boon each. Kadru wished for one thousand sons, mighty and invincible nagas. Vinata chose to have two sons who would be far greater than Kadru's. Kashyapa went away to concentrate on his meditation and ascetic practices – standing on one leg and gazing at the sun, immersing himself in water up to his neck, living only on air – to gain more and more spiritual powers.

Soon Kadru produced one thousand eggs. And Vinata produced two. The sisters looked after their eggs carefully, bathing them in warm water, cleaning the fragile shells every day, waiting, waiting, waiting for the first crack to appear. The thousand eggs hatched first, each producing a slithery glistening snake, whose rippling body made the sunlight dance on its scales. All the snakes in the world are descended from the sons of Kadru. She was delighted and mocked her sister whose eggs were as firm and smooth as the day they had been produced.

Vinata was not happy and, in a moment of envy, she broke open one of her two eggs. A sad, half-formed creature emerged. The top half of his body was glorious – he had a sharp and proud beak, piercing eyes, great shoulders and magnificent iridescent wings, shining with colours that only the mind could imagine. He was every inch a massive bird. Until you came to his legs – they were small and weak and unshapely. They trembled as he tried to stand, unable to take the weight of the body they were expected to carry. The almost-bird was enraged at his mother's impatience that had brought him into the world too soon. He cursed his mother – she would be her sister's slave for years and years and years and eventually, it would be her second son who would free her from her bondage.

He flapped his great wings that shone with many colours and flew into the sky – higher and higher until he was high enough to reach the sun. There he became the herald of the dawn and was named Aruna. We see him every day as he paints the sky in shades of red and yellow and orange and pink, sometimes even a little lavender, before the Sun rises and climbs into his chariot to circle the world. Aruna drives the chariot yoked with the Sun's seven horses, standing in front of this bright god, so full of heat and energy, tempering them before they reach the earth.

Vinata shed bitter tears, but there was nothing she could do to bring her son back. As time passed, she taught herself patience since that was a virtue she lacked. It took five hundred long years for Vinata's second egg to break open. And when it did, a great bird emerged, perfect in wing and limb. After a quick look at his mother, Suparna, he of the fine feathers, flew off in search of food.

Around that time, the gods and the asuras

had churned the ocean and among the many marvellous things and creatures that emerged from that great upheaval, was Ucchaihshravas, the horse with the pricked-up ears.* Together, the sisters, Vinata and Kadru, admired this horse who had no equal in the three worlds.

Kadru said, 'What colour is this horse, dear sister?'

'White, of course,' said Vinata. 'He was born from the ocean of milk. He is completely and purely white.'

'I say he's not,' said Kadru. 'There must be some black somewhere on his body. Shall we take a bet? If the horse is not as white as you say, then you shall be my slave. And if I am wrong, I shall work for you with no complaints.'

Vinata agreed and the sisters decided to view the horse from close quarters. But before they set off, Kadru called her one thousand sons, the great nagas, and said to them, 'I have taken a bet that the horse Ucchaihshravas is not entirely white. I cannot be wrong. If I lose, I will become a servant to my sister. I will not live like that. Go

---

* See the story 'The Churning of the Ocean' on page 1.

to Ucchaihshravas and wrap yourselves around his tail so that he is not perfectly white.'

Some of Kadru's sons were horrified and said they could not do something so deceitful. They refused to obey their mother. Kadru's anger knew no bounds and she cursed the sons who would not do as she asked. 'You will die, horribly and in pain, burning and twisting and shrieking in the fire of a king's snake sacrifice!' Kadru's other sons heard that terrible curse and decided they should fulfil their mother's wishes. They went and inserted themselves into the horse's tail, lying still and silent, as if they were hair.

Meanwhile, the sisters approached the perfect horse and examined him closely. They checked his pricked-up ears, they stroked his long arched neck and lifted his glossy mane, they even searched his taut belly and looked at his cloven hooves, one by one.

Vinata said triumphantly, 'See? White! Whiter than white! Not a speck on him, not a dot, not a spot, not a shadow! Come sister, be my slave!'

'Not so quick, my sweet-smiling one,' said Kadru. 'We haven't looked at his tail yet.' She lifted the horse's tail and shouted, 'Aha! See here!

There are some dark hair. They're black! The horse is not white, not from the tip of his nose to the tip of his tail! You be my slave, sister, and the slave of my children too!'

When Suparna, who is better known to us as Garuda, heard what had happened, he decided that he, too, would serve Kadru and her sons to lighten his mother's burden. Oh, how Kadru and her snaky children enjoyed tormenting Vinata and Garuda. 'Take us here!' they would command. 'Now take us there, as high as the sun!' 'We want to see the ocean made of salt! We want to visit the island in the middle of the sweet-water sea!' they cried. Finally, Garuda asked his cousins what they would take in exchange for Vinata's freedom. In a flash, the snakes said they wanted to drink amrita, the divine potion which would make them immortal.

Garuda set off to fetch the nectar of immortality. Along the way, he was overcome by a great hunger. As he flew along, he swallowed thousands of forest-dwelling Nishadas, but they made not the slightest dent in his hunger. Then he flew to where a massive elephant and a tortoise were engaged in constant combat (they had been brothers in their previous life and had fought over money and so now, they were condemned to fight each other for a long, long time). Garuda swooped down and plucked them from the ground in his great claws. He flew onwards, looking for a place where he might eat them at leisure. He noticed a huge tree that seemed strong enough to bear his weight, and he spiralled down towards it, his great wings riding the currents of the air.

As he was about to alight on the tree, he noticed that there were hundreds of tiny rishis clinging to one of its branches. 'Help, help!' they squeaked in their little voices. 'We are the Valakhilyas. We are trapped here. Take us home!' Garuda felt sorry for the little sages so he put his hunger aside and broke off the branch. He carried it in his beak and laid it gently down on the earth so that the Valakhilyas could find their way home. Finally, he reached Mount Gandhamadana and devoured the elephant and the tortoise he had been holding in his claws all this time.

At last, Garuda was able to concentrate on his task of bringing the amrita back to Kadru's sons. But the gods guarded the amrita fiercely. They had placed it in a huge ring of fire that touched the sky.

If you managed to get past that, you encountered an enormous wheel with rotating blades. And if you slipped through that, you met gigantic serpents, one on each side of the pot of amrita. Garuda sucked up the waters of the ocean and spat them out to douse the fire. Then he reduced himself to a tiny bird and flew through the metal contraption. And finally, he ripped the serpents apart with his sharp beak and claws. He picked up the pot and flew back towards his waiting cousins, the snakes.

Vishnu was very impressed with the great bird and his cleverness. He stopped him and said, 'I can make you immortal even without the amrita!' Garuda replied, 'Then I shall be with you forever, I will carry you wherever you want to go!' and he flew onwards. Indra was not so pleased and promised Garuda serpents as food for the rest of his life if only he would give the amrita back to the gods. 'Let me take this back to the sons of Kadru so that my mother can be free. Then I will give you all that is left,' said Garuda.

Garuda delivered the amrita to Kadru's sons and placed it on the sacred kusha grass in front of them. 'Let my mother go. She need no longer be your slave,' he said. Kadru and her sons agreed and eagerly reached for the pot. 'You must bathe and purify yourselves before you drink this divine substance,' Garuda said to them. The snakes slithered off. Indra had been following Garuda anxiously all this while and in a trice, he swooped down and grabbed the pot. When the snakes came back, there were only a few drops of amrita scattered on the grass, spilled from when Indra had taken the pot away in such haste. In desperation, Kadru's sons licked at the grass furiously, trying to get as much of the amrita as they could. They didn't get much, but the sharp blades of grass split their tongues. That's why snakes have forked tongues even today. They shed their old skin and grow new skin as a tiny measure of immortality that the drops of amrita bestowed upon them.

Garuda ate snakes to his heart's content and lived happily with his mother. But he kept his promise and he is famous in the three worlds as Vishnu's vehicle.

3

Bhagiratha Brings Ganga to the Earth

Long ago, a king named Sagara decided to perform the ashwamedha, the great horse sacrifice, to make the gods happy and to establish himself as the mightiest of all kings on earth. Indra, king of the gods, was afraid that Sagara would become powerful enough to attack his own throne in heaven. So he stole the horse from the sacrifice that Sagara was conducting and hid it. The sacrifice could not be completed, but though Sagara remained honoured and respected by the people, he did not forget what Indra had done.

Sagara had two wives and a sage had promised him that one of his wives would have one son while the other would have sixty thousand sons. It turned out exactly as the sage had prophesied. The single son was a nasty fellow with a foul temper and bad habits, and Sagara soon gave up on him. The other sixty thousand were no better. They too were quick to anger and often acted without much thought. But they were obedient to their father and respected his wishes and commands. As soon as they were old enough, Sagara told the sixty thousand what had happened at his sacrifice and sent them off to find the missing horse.

The sixty thousand sons searched every corner of the earth but the horse was nowhere to be found. Then they began to dig into the underworld, deeper and deeper until they could go no further. Here too they searched in all directions – north, south, east and west. They came across the massive elephants who guarded each of the four quarters of the world but there was no horse. Finally, when they were utterly exhausted and ready to give up, they found the sacrificial horse grazing quietly, tethered next to the sage Kapila who was deep in meditation.

Sagara's sons thought that the sage was the one who had stolen the horse and without waiting to find out more, they taunted him and insulted him, calling him a thief and a robber. Kapila was enraged. He opened one of his eyes and a huge flame shot out. Kapila burned the sixty thousand sons of Sagara to ashes with that single glance.

The souls of those sixty thousand sons wandered through the universe, unable to find peace because no one had been able to perform their funeral rites. Generations of Sagara's descendants prayed to the gods, they beseeched Brahma and pleaded for his help in this matter, but their prayers remained fruitless.

At long last, Bhagiratha was born in Sagara's royal line. He was proud and brave, and a good king, but despite his many virtues, he did not have a son. He was also determined to bring peace to the souls of Sagara's sixty thousand sons, his forefathers. And so, Bhagiratha embarked on a series of austerities so that he could obtain boons from the gods.

Braving the scorching heat of summer and the biting cold of winter and the onslaught of the rains, he stood in a circle of five fires with his arms raised above his head. He ate only once a month. He stayed like this for one thousand years, until Brahma came to him and said, 'I am pleased with you, my child. Ask me for a boon!'

Bhagiratha replied, 'I want to complete the funeral rites for Sagara's sons, my ancestors. I want to scatter their ashes in the waters of the Ganga. Make that possible, if I have pleased you. And also, give me a son so that our royal line does not end with me!'

Brahma smiled and said, 'Ganga lives in the sky, where she is the river of the heavens. You will have to persuade her to come down to earth. But I fear that the earth will not be able to bear the force of her descent. Ask Shiva, the holder of the trident, to help you.'

Bhagiratha was not to be distracted from his mission to honour the souls of his ancestors and decided that he would now attract the attention of Shiva. He stayed where he was, continuing his formidable penance. With the big toe on his right foot, he pressed down hard on the earth and stood like that for one hundred years. At this point, Shiva appeared and said, 'I will help you, Bhagiratha! I will make sure that Ganga listens to your request and comes to earth so that you can fulfil the promise you have made to your forefathers. And so that the gentle earth is not harmed, I shall bear the force of Ganga's descent on my head as she falls from the heavens.'

Involved against her will in the plans of the great gods, Ganga turned into a mighty river and, roaring and rushing, she descended from the sky on to Shiva's head. She was not at all pleased with what she had been forced to do and, to punish Shiva for his part, she planned to sweep him off into the underworld with the power of her fast-flowing streams. But Shiva knew her thoughts and when Ganga fell on to his head, he captured her in his twisted, curled and matted locks. Ganga got lost in his hair, unable to make her way through the knots and tangles and twists and turns. Shiva wanted to keep Ganga hidden because he did not want his wife, Parvati, to be jealous. As a result, Ganga became more and more confused as she wandered around in Shiva's hair and was trapped there for many, many years.

Meanwhile, Bhagiratha could see no sign of the heavenly river on earth. He performed even more severe austerities to please Shiva and finally, Shiva let Ganga fall into the Bindusaras lake. What a commotion there was when the roaring waters burst out from Shiva's hair! Gods and gandharvas, siddhas and charanas, the sages and the great serpents, all gathered to watch as Ganga came pouring forth. The energy and brilliance of the gods and the other sky-dwellers lit up the three worlds and their light sparkled like diamonds on the rushing water. Fish of all shapes and sizes and large and small water creatures that lived in the depths of the river flashed silver and gold, like streaks of lightning, as they were tossed about by the descending waters that thundered and splashed and crashed against rocks and stones. Spray filled the air like rain from monsoon clouds.

Ganga's waters divided into streams as they hit the earth – some streams were calm and flowed smoothly, others rushed along, uprooting grass and plants and pulling them into their turbulent waters, still other streams flowed slowly in great loops and graceful curves. Some rose in great waves, others stayed close to the ground. Everywhere, in whatever stream, the waters that fell from Shiva's head were cool and as clear as crystal. They purified everything that they touched.

Ganga split herself into seven streams – three of them flowed in an eastern direction and three flowed west. The seventh stream followed Bhagiratha wherever he went. The king climbed into his chariot and the stream flowed behind him. The gods and gandharvas and many others who lived in the skies came along with Ganga because they were fond of her – she had been their river in heaven and she had given them much joy.

Bhagiratha drove his chariot all the way to the shore of the salty ocean and Ganga came with him. As he scattered the ashes of his ancestors into the waves, Ganga merged with the salt waters. The king finished his rituals and with his palms joined, he bowed his head and purified himself.

When he opened his eyes and looked up, Brahma was standing before him, once again. 'You have been successful, Bhagiratha – you have brought this river, pure of water and beloved to the gods, to earth for the benefit of all living beings who dwell in this realm. Long after you have left the earth, you will be remembered and honoured for your determination and your great deed. Ganga will be named after you. She will be called Bhagirathi because she is like your daughter, she

is on earth because of you. Moreover, as long as Ganga flows on earth, so long shall your ancestors stay in heaven.'

Brahma blessed the king and went back to where he had come from. Bhagiratha thanked all the gods and went back to rule his kingdom, well pleased with what he had done. In time, a son was born to him and Sagara's royal line produced many virtuous kings who ruled the earth wisely and well.

4

The Magic Cow

Once, long ago, there was a cow who could make all the wishes of her owner come true. She could produce food, drink, clothes, jewels, even horses and warriors, anything at all that her owner asked her for. Her name was Kamadhenu. Some say she was born, along with so many other wondrous things, when the gods and the asuras churned the great ocean. Others say she was the daughter of Brahma himself, though many believed she was the daughter of Daksha. Or Kashyapa.

At the start of this story, Kamadhenu lived with the great sage Vasishtha and his wife. They loved her as if she was their own child and had named her Shabala, because her body was sweetly dappled with different colours. They made sure that she was always comfortable and well fed. Vasishtha was known for his great spiritual powers but like many other sages, he lived a simple life on the edge of the forest in a small compound with a few students. Their huts were thatched, they collected their water from the river nearby and grew a few crops, enough to feed them all, but not much more than that.

One day, a mighty king named Vishwamitra came to that same forest on a royal hunt. A royal hunt meant that many of the king's courtiers and soldiers came with him. It also meant that hundreds of animals and birds – deer and boars and lions and tigers and ducks and geese and partridges – would be killed and taken back to the palace for a grand feast. And so, while there were horses and elephants and many kinds of weapons and whistles and horns and drums, the royal party was not carrying much food.

It was a hot day and soon the king was both hungry and thirsty. His companions knew that they were close to Vasishtha's settlement and they led the king in that direction, to the edge of the forest. Vishwamitra noticed how small and simple the sage's home was and he said to his men, 'It is the sage's duty to offer us hospitality. But he will never be able to feed us all, there are so many of us. I will go to him with just a few of you. The rest can stay here. I don't want to embarrass the great man.'

Vishwamitra approached Vasishtha's hut and called out to him. At once, the sage and his wife appeared, carrying water to welcome the king and for him to wash his feet. 'Come, your majesty. Make yourself comfortable. We will soon have a meal ready for you,' said Vasishtha.

'I don't want to trouble you, good sir,' said the king. 'Whatever you are eating will suit me as well.'

Before the king's startled eyes, the sage's students started to lay out plates that shone like gold. They carried huge pots that smelled as if the gods themselves had been cooking for the sage and his wife. Vasishtha said, 'Majesty, surely you have more courtiers and soldiers with you. Please, invite them all to eat. As you can see, there is more than enough food.'

The sage instructed one of his students to bring all the king's men to the meal and when they

were seated, the biggest and the most sumptuous banquet they had ever seen was laid before them, replete with all the six flavours. There were mounds of fluffy rice and soft wheat breads, there were pickles and condiments and there were meats and sauces and cooked vegetables and fresh fruit. There were juices made from flowers and all kinds of delectable things made from milk. There was butter and ghee and curds and sweetmeats that were like nectar. And though all the king's men and the king himself ate and ate and ate some more, the food kept coming. The students served the guests tirelessly with smiles on their faces.

Finally, when Vishwamitra could eat no more, he said, 'Blessed sir, how did you manage such a feast? I see a tiny kitchen and just a few crops growing outside your hut. Surely your good wife could not have produced this feast on her own. I have not eaten food like this even in my own palace!'

Vasishtha smiled and said, 'We are lucky to have Shabala, our beloved cow. We treat her as we would our own child and she provides us with whatever we need.'

'A cow did all this,' stuttered Vishwamitra.

'What kind of cow? I can believe that she gives you milk and butter and cheese for your table and manure for your fields so that your grains and vegetables grow strong and sweet. Perhaps you even sacrifice her children for a meal when you have guests. But all this!'

'She is a gift from the gods, my lord,' said Vasishtha. 'She fulfils our wishes, she gives us whatever we ask for.'

'Can she produce gold and jewels as well?' asked the king.

'I have never had need for those, but I'm sure she can if she is asked,' replied the sage.

'Ah, but such a cow is far better suited for a king, surely,' said Vishwamitra. 'You have no need for gold and jewels, for fine food and drink. Your needs are simple, you don't need a magic cow to fulfil them. Give your cow to me, sage. I will give you anything you want in exchange.'

'How can I give you Shabala? She is like our child,' said the sage. 'Who sells their children, good king?'

'She's not your child. She is a cow. Anyone can own her. Prepare yourself, sage, I am going to take her with me when I leave. I can give you a thousand ordinary cows, I will give you horses and elephants decked with gold. I will give mountains of bright jewels. I will give you more wealth than you can imagine. But I will take your cow!'

'But, your majesty, Shabala is an important part of my rituals and all that I must give away after they are completed. I cannot perform my sacred duties without her!' cried Vasishtha.

His wife came out when she heard the raised voice. She fell at the king's feet, weeping, and begged him not to take Shabala away.

But the king retorted, 'I have a hundred sons and thousands of warriors, try and stop me!'

Vishwamitra ordered his men to seize Shabala by force. The soldiers pushed their way past the terrified students and ran to where Shabala was grazing on sweet hay. She looked up when she heard the commotion and in a second, the soldiers had grabbed her by the neck.

As they tried to drag her towards the king, Shabala cried out in a piteous voice, 'Father Vasishtha! Where are you? What is happening?'

Vasishtha came running to her and stroked her face and neck. 'O my child, the king Vishwamitra wants to take you away from us! He thinks he has far greater need of you than we do. There is nothing I can do to stop him, his men are armed and they are all skilled warriors.'

Shabala tossed her head and spoke firmly, 'Father, Mother, do you want the king to take me away? Tell me, truly!'

Vasishtha and his wife wept as they shook their heads and looked at the ground, helpless in front of the king's might.

Suddenly, Shabala was transformed. She cast aside her sweet, gentle nature and bellowed, 'Let go of me!' in a voice that shook the earth. The soldiers holding her trembled but they did not loosen their grip on her.

Shabala shook herself and roared. Out of her mouth came hundreds and hundreds of warriors, armed with swords and shields. From her hooves came another thousand archers, their bows and arrows at the ready. Lancers and spearmen and horsemen came forth from her horns and soon, there was an entire army prepared to protect her. They set upon the king's men, the soldiers as well as the courtiers, and a great battle ensued.

Vishwamitra himself entered the fray, willing to go to any lengths to capture the cow he so desired.

As Shabala's warriors were crushed by the king's men, more poured forth from her body and the pores of her skin.

Finally, Vishwamitra had to admit that he had been defeated. He was not at all pleased but still, he bowed to Vasishtha and said, 'Keep your cow, great sage. Clearly, this is not the time for me to have her. But I will not forget this, my powers as a king have been challenged. You are forever my sworn enemy and I will have my revenge,' he said, his voice shaking with anger.

Vasishtha and his wife wept tears of joy as they caressed and embraced their beloved Shabala. 'Go, Vishwamitra,' said Vasishtha. 'Go back to your city and your palace and your treasury and your wars and your wives. We are happy here with our simple lives and our simple needs.'

On his way back to the city, Vishwamitra could think of nothing but his humiliating defeat. 'Surely the powers of a sage are greater than those of a king,' he thought to himself. 'What is the use of being a king when a sage who lives in the forest, who has nothing, is given a cow that can produce food and wealth and mighty warriors? I want to become that – a man so powerful that the gods make sure he is pleased even when he does nothing.'

By the time he entered his palace, Vishwamitra had made up his mind. 'I will renounce this kingship and I will undertake the greatest of all austerities. I, too, will become a sage and then I will truly be Vasishtha's equal.'

Meanwhile in the forest, Vasishtha and his wife and their students and gentle Shabala went back to the life they had known before it was so rudely interrupted by Vishwamitra.

5

Takshaka's Revenge

Long ago, there was a king named Shwetaki who performed sacrifices continuously for twelve long years. When he died, he went to heaven, but Agni, god of fire, Eater of All, who had consumed all the ghee that was offered into the fire for those twelve years, felt terribly ill. His stomach hurt and he could not bear the idea of eating another thing. Agni went to Grandfather Brahma and complained about his condition. Brahma reassured him and said, 'There is a cure for your upset stomach, Agni. Burn the Khandava forest. When you eat the fat of all the animals and birds and snakes that live there, it will counteract all this ghee in your system and you will feel better.'

Meanwhile on earth, the five Pandava brothers had been given land on which to establish their new city. It lay to the east of the river Yamuna and was covered with a dense forest, which happened to be the Khandava. They would have to clear it before they could think of building anything. When Arjuna and his friend Krishna were planning how they would go about this, they were approached by a stranger.

His hair was red, his eyes were fiery, he seemed to glow, and sparks flew from his feet when he walked. 'I am hungry all the time,' he said to them. 'No matter what I eat, I cannot fill my stomach. Help me!'

Arjuna replied, 'Tell me what you want to eat and I will bring it for you.'

'I am Agni,' the man replied. 'I need to devour the Khandava forest. I can do that quite easily, but Indra, god of the storm, and Wielder of the Thunderbolt, has a friend who lives there. His name is Takshaka and he is a snake. Every time I set the forest alight, Indra sends the rains to douse my flames.'

'We will protect you as you burn the forest,'

offered Arjuna. 'But we will need weapons to drive away the clouds and the rain. I will need a bow that will release my arrows as fast as I shoot them, a quiver that would never run out of arrows and a chariot that moves as quickly as thought despite being loaded with weapons. Its wheels must rumble like thunder and the horses that draw it must be swifter than the wind.'

Agni said that he would supply the weapons that Arjuna needed. He gave him his own chariot which was faster than any other in the three worlds, yoked with horses that were as white as summer clouds. The chariot's flag was decorated with an enormous ape, his mouth open in a silent but ferocious battle cry.*

For Arjuna, the finest archer in the three worlds, Agni asked his friend Varuna, god of the waters, for the magnificent Gandiva bow that rivalled Pinaka, the bow of Shiva. For Krishna, Agni brought the deadly discus, Sudarshana, that would never miss its mark and would return immediately to Krishna's hand.

---

*If you want to know why Arjuna had an ape on his flag, read 'When Bhima Met His Brother' on page 133.

The two friends were now ready to help Agni burn down the forest. This plan suited them as well, for it would clear the land on which they could build the new Pandava capital.

'Go, Agni! Burn the Khandava, eat as much as you want, let your hunger be satisfied!' shouted Arjuna as he whipped his horses and surged forward in his chariot.

Agni transformed himself into Fire and roared into the forest. Khandava blazed from every side, sending plumes of thick smoke into the air. Krishna and Arjuna placed themselves at each end of the forest and began the massacre of all the creatures that lived there.

Arjuna's arrows felled the birds that flew into the sky to escape the flames. Krishna went after the animals that fled on land to get away from the searing heat. Everywhere and in all directions, elephants, tigers, lions, deer, boar, jackals, hyenas, wolves and bison wailed and howled and bellowed and screamed and cried. Some clung to their young ones, trying to protect them, others died gasping for breath as their lungs exploded, holding on to their families whom they could not bear to leave.

Blood boiled, eyes popped out of heads, feathers were scorched, bodies were roasted, limbs were charred, fat bubbled and bones and muscles snapped in the heat. Never had Agni been so hungry, never had Fire devoured so much with so much pleasure.

Indra realized what was happening and as quickly as he could, he sent his storm winds to drive the biggest, heaviest rain clouds over Khandava. Rain poured down upon the blaze and the flames sizzled, as if they were about to die out. But Arjuna knew Indra's tricks and he also had knowledge of all his weapons. He loosed arrows so fast and thick that they formed a shield above and around the forest, keeping out the rain from Indra's thundering black clouds which were lit by streaks of golden lightning. The shield also prevented animals from escaping and more and more of them were killed.

Indra's friend, the snake Takshaka, was not in the forest at the time but his wife and his son were both there. His wife tried to swallow her son, Ashwasena, to keep him safe, but Arjuna's arrow sliced off her head. Indra tried to save his friend's son and sent a howling, raging blast of wind that knocked Arjuna unconscious for a few moments. Ashwasena slithered away to safety.

Arjuna's weapons and skills defeated Indra, and the god of the storm retired to heaven.

Khandava burned and burned for six, seven, eight, nine, ten whole days and Arjuna and Krishna kept up the slaughter of all the living creatures that dwelt there. Finally, when there was nothing left, when not a single blade of grass was standing, Agni's hunger was satisfied and the fire died down, leaving a charred and barren land. Agni gave the weapons he had gathered from the gods to Arjuna and Krishna as a reward for their help.

Takshaka was Indra's friend and though he knew that Arjuna was Indra's son, he vowed to take revenge on the man who had killed his beloved wife. He waited patiently, knowing that snakes outlive humans and that his time to strike would come.

Long years later, after many people had lived and loved and died, including Arjuna and Krishna, Arjuna's grandson, Parikshit, became king in the lands around the area where the Khandava forest used to be. Once, when Parikshit was out hunting, he got separated from his companions. He was overcome with thirst and he stumbled upon a sage's hermitage. He looked around and all he could see was the sage, deep in meditation. He begged him for water, but the sage had taken a vow of silence and ignored the king.

Parikshit was incensed. He saw a dead snake lying in the grass. He lifted it with the tip of his bow and placed it around the sage's neck. The sage remained calm and silent but when his son returned and saw the insult to his father, he cursed Parikshit – that the king would die of a snakebite within seven days.

The sage was not pleased with his son's reaction for he believed that an ascetic needed to control his anger. Besides, he knew Parikshit to be a good and wise king, for the most part. He sent a message to Parikshit about the curse and urged him to protect himself.

Parikshit grew very anxious when he heard this and within a day, he had a beautiful new palace constructed for himself. It stood on an immensely high pillar which was surrounded by a moat which was surrounded by circles of priests reciting anti-snake spells and performing anti-snake rituals.

Parikshit heaved a sigh of relief for the palace was filled with other priests who knew how to counteract snake venom. Nonetheless, for six days Parikshit slept little and ate even less despite the fact that all his food and everything that came into the palace was thoroughly checked.

Takshaka had heard about the curse and was counting the days. He disguised himself as an ascetic and along with a group of other snakes also in disguise, he made his way to Parikshit's city and his new palace. When the snakes got there, they mingled with the other ascetics and priests who had come to protect the king and joined them in the dining areas where everyone was fed. In the blink of an eye, Takshaka transformed himself into a tiny worm. He slipped into the kitchen and slid into a fruit that was being sent to the king's chambers.

It was the evening of the sixth day and Parikshit was becoming less fearful as the deadline for the curse seemed to be running out. He was in a cheerful mood and joked with his companions as he ate the fresh fruit that had been brought to him. He noticed a worm in the tray and laughing, he said, 'Oho! This little worm must be the snake that has come to kill me! Let's see what it can do!' He picked up the worm and placed it on his neck. Silent but deadly, Takshaka emerged from the worm and sank his fangs into Parikshit's neck, filling his body with a poison that had no antidote. In seconds, the king was dead and Takshaka had vanished. And so it was that Takshaka avenged the killing of his wife and son many generations later. But the Khandava forest has been destroyed forever.

6

Shukra and Kacha

The gods and the asuras were enemies, even though they were both born from the sage Kashyapa. The gods lived in the realms above the earth and the asuras in the realms below, but they fought each other for supremacy of the three worlds. Sometimes the gods won and sometimes the asuras won but this constant fighting was exhausting. Both sides tried hard to make themselves so strong that the other side would not even try and attack them.

The teacher of the gods was Brihaspati, born of the first light in the world. He was a wise and learned brahmin and had a calm temperament. The asuras also had a teacher who was as learned as Brihaspati but was more powerful. This brahmin's name was Shukra, though he was also known in the three worlds as Ushanas.

Shukra had a special knowledge that no one else had – he knew the secret of bringing the dead back to life. This was an invaluable secret because it meant that whenever the asuras were killed in battle with the gods, he could bring them back to life. The numbers of the asuras never diminished and this made them stronger than the gods in times of war.

The gods desperately wanted to have this secret so that they could be equal to the asuras. They plotted and planned and thought about this scheme and that, but Shukra was loyal to the asuras and kept this knowledge entirely to himself.

Finally, the gods went to Kacha, Brihaspati's son and said to him, 'Shukra will believe you if you go to him and say that you have left your father because you wish to learn from the greater of the two teachers. Learn the secret of bringing the dead back to life and then come back to us. Shukra has a beautiful daughter, you can win her over as well and she will help you get the secret from her father.'

Kacha agreed and presented himself before Shukra. He bowed low and introduced himself, saying that he had come in search of the ultimate knowledge. Shukra accepted him as a student and Kacha began to live in the teacher's hermitage along with all the other students. He treated Devayani, Shukra's lovely daughter, with utmost respect. He helped her with her household chores, he gathered firewood for her, he plucked rare flowers from unreachable trees that were deep in the forest and brought them to her to tie in her hair.

Slowly but surely, Devayani began to fall in love with the young man who had come to her father from the gods. At the same time, her father, too, felt that Kacha was a special student and taught him things that he had kept away from others.

One day, Kacha had taken Shukra's cows into the forest to graze. A group of asuras was also in the forest at that time and, seeing the son of Brihaspati, they fell upon him and killed him. They cut his body up into tiny pieces and fed them to

the jackals. The cows wandered home sadly at the end of the day, without their cowherd.

When Devayani saw the cows without Kacha she began to cry and went running to her father. 'Something has happened to Kacha,' she wailed. 'Look, the cows have come home without him!' Shukra could not bear to see his daughter so upset and he, too, loved the young man who was now missing. He used his divine vision and saw what had happened to Kacha and how the jackals had eaten the pieces of his body.

'Calm yourself, my dear,' he said to Devayani. 'Kacha has been killed by some foolish and violent asuras. But I can restore him to life.'

Shukra went into deep meditation and recalled the magic verses that could bring the dead back to life. He muttered them to himself and sprinkled sacred water on the ground in front of him. Almost immediately, Kacha came running out of the forest, as hale and hearty as he had been in the morning when he took the cows out to graze. 'A group of asuras killed me,' he panted. 'But thanks to you, dear teacher, I am alive and well again!'

Life returned to normal and Kacha continued to learn and go into the forest every day for various reasons. Once, when he was collecting flowers for Devayani, the same group of asuras saw him. They knew about Shukra's special powers and realized that the teacher had brought Kacha back to life. They killed him again, but this time, they made sure that no traces of his body remained. They ground up his body into a fine powder and dissolved it in a pot of wine.

Then they took the pot of wine and called on Shukra, offering it to him as a gift. Although Shukra did not usually drink wine, the asuras flattered him and cajoled him and eventually, they got him to drink the entire pot. Shukra fell over, quite drunk, and the asuras went on their way, sure that this time they had destroyed Kacha, the son of Brihaspati, teacher of the gods.

Again, it was Devayani who noticed that Kacha had not returned from the forest even though it had become dark. She ran to her father and shook him awake. 'They have done it, again. Kacha has not returned. I am sure the asuras have attacked and killed him. Bring him back, Father, I beg you. I cannot live without Kacha!'

Shukra shook his head sadly and said, 'I have brought him back to life once. I cannot do it again.

Forget about him. You have the world at your feet – you are beautiful, I am powerful, anyone would be happy to marry you. I cannot bring back to life a man who has been killed twice.'

Devayani threw herself upon the ground and began to weep inconsolably. 'I cannot live without him. I want to die. I will stop eating, I will starve myself to death because the world without Kacha is nothing to me!'

Shukra knew that his daughter could be very stubborn and was perfectly capable of starving herself to death before his very eyes. He wailed aloud, 'Oh, these asuras must hate me – they keep murdering my students. Now they have killed Kacha who is a brahmin. No one can get away with that, not even Indra! Kacha, my dear Kacha, I wish you were here!'

From deep inside Shukra's stomach came a small voice. 'I am here, I am in your stomach!'

Shukra fell down in shock. 'Where? In my stomach? How did you get there?' he stammered.

'I am alive because of the power of my own austerities,' said Kacha. 'I remember everything that happened to me. Listen, and I will tell you. The asuras caught me while I was gathering flowers for your daughter. They beat me and stabbed me and punched and kicked me. I can remember the pain. Then they burned me and crushed me into a fine powder which they mixed in the wine they brought for you. You drank it. That is how I am in your stomach.'

Shukra looked at his daughter and said, 'I know you love this boy, that you cannot live without him. Cut open my stomach and let him out. I shall die so that Kacha can live.'

'O Father, do not ask this of me,' wailed Devayani. 'I love Kacha but I cannot live without you either. You are both father and mother to me!'

Shukra thought for a moment and then said, 'There is one way that both Kacha and I can be alive and in this world. Listen carefully, Kacha. I will teach you the secret incantations for bringing the dead back to life. After you have learned them, rip open my stomach from the inside. When you come out of my body alive, you can revive me with the same secret formula and I, too, will come back to life.'

Kacha readily agreed and Shukra began to teach him the secret. Slowly, Kacha became ready to use the same power himself. He ripped his way out of his teacher's belly and stood before Devayani, as young and handsome as he had ever been.

'Let us not waste time,' said Kacha. He bent over Shukra's body and quickly muttered the magic words, sprinkling water around himself. Shukra's stomach closed up and he came back to life.

He embraced Kacha and said, 'You are not only my greatest student, you are now also my son as you have emerged from my body!' Kacha bent and touched Shukra's feet and called him father.

Kacha continued to live in the hermitage as before but he knew that soon it would be time for him to return to his own father and to the realm of the gods with the secret he had gained from Shukra. When it was time for him to leave, he bowed low before his teacher and thanked him for all that he had learned. Shukra had tears in his eyes but he knew that every student must leave his teacher and go out into the world.

Kacha went to Devayani to say goodbye, but she begged him to stay. She said, 'You know I love you, Kacha. Stay here. Marry me. This is your home, more than the place that you came from!'

She came forward and placed her hand on his arm.

Kacha recoiled in horror. 'Get away from me. How can you think this? I am your brother, in spirit and in the flesh. I cannot marry you!'

'But surely you love me, you have always been so kind to me!' wept Devayani.

'I have never loved you,' retorted Kacha. 'All that I did for you, I did from a sense of duty. You are the daughter of my teacher. I am duty-bound to respect you.'

Devayani's eyes blazed with anger. She looked directly at Kacha and said, 'I will never forget this insult. You will forget whatever you have learned from my father, especially the power to bring the dead back to life. These last few years of your life will have been lived in vain. You have gained nothing from them, not even a loving wife!'

Kacha was horrified and could not control the anger that rose up within him. 'I curse you too. May you never have a worthy husband. Whoever you marry will be spineless!' Then he turned his back on Devayani and returned to Brihaspati and the gods.

7

Jambavan, King of the Bears

Once, when Bali, king of the asuras, ruled the three worlds, a brahmin dwarf approached him in his court. Bali was a good and just king who performed his duties with ease and grace and so, he honoured the brahmin and said, 'Good sir, who are you and what can I do for you? Ask me for anything, it is my duty as a king to give it to you.'

The little dwarf said, 'I am Vamana. Give me as much of the earth as I can cover in three strides.'

Bali smiled and said, 'Of course,' not knowing that the dwarf was Vishnu who had come to reclaim the three worlds for the gods.

Before Bali's astonished eyes, Vamana grew in size till he touched the skies. With one stride, he covered the entire earth and the whole of the heavens. With his second stride, he covered the underworld and all its creatures. 'Where shall I place my foot for my third stride?' he asked Bali.

The king bowed his head low and said, 'Blessed one, place your foot on my head. That way, you will have conquered me as well as the three worlds.'

The gods rejoiced and all of Bali's courtiers praised their king. Among the creatures present in Bali's court that day was a bear named Jambavan. He clapped and sang and he beat his drum loudly and with great enthusiasm as Vamana was taking his three strides. As Vamana raised his leg for the second stride, his foot hit Jambavan on the shoulder. The bear fell to the ground, stunned. He soon recovered from this accidental blow but he knew he would never have the same strength in his arms again.

Jambavan retired to the forest where he lived on roots and fruits and took care of his people because he was, in fact, the king of the bears. As he grew old, he was respected for his wisdom and for the stories he could tell, for he had seen and heard many things in his long years on earth.

Jambavan was a friend and ally to the monkeys of Kishkindha and they often took his advice on various matters. When Sugriva called all the mighty monkeys together to begin the search for Rama's wife, Sita, he invited Jambavan to join them. Jambavan was asked to go south with the search party which was under the command of Hanuman, the greatest of all monkeys. Jambavan kept mostly to himself as they went deeper and deeper into unknown lands. But the monkeys knew he was there and that was a comfort to them.

Eventually, the monkeys could go no further because they had reached the shores of the ocean. They had never seen the ocean before and were terrified of its waves that rose up high and then crashed to the shore. As the monkeys lay on the sand, ready to give up their lives because they could not disappoint Rama and Sugriva, they were approached by a great bird, Sampati, who had lost his wings by flying too close to the sun. Sampati told the monkeys he had seen a woman being

carried across the skies to an island that lay in the middle of the ocean, an island that was impossible to reach unless one had wings.

The monkeys gathered around, boasting of their capacity to leap across miles and miles, as if they were, in fact, flying. But none of them could quite manage the distance to the island, which was a full one hundred yojanas, much more than a hundred miles.

Quietly, Jambavan spoke. He said, 'There is one monkey here who can make this enormous leap. And yet he remains silent. Hanuman, why don't you say something?'

'What shall I say, Jambavan? I can't leap any further than the others,' said Hanuman.

'Listen,' said Jambavan. 'Let me tell you who you really are and what you can do,' and he told Hanuman the story of who he was and what his great powers were. Hanuman took inspiration and leapt over the ocean to the island. That was the beginning of the end for the rakshasas who lived there. Soon, they were defeated by the brave monkeys, their king, Ravana, was killed and Rama got his wife back.

After he had helped the monkeys win the war

against the rakshasas, Jambavan went back to his cave in the forest, to the quiet life that he loved best. The fur on his snout was now touched with grey, but his eyes were sharp and bright and his hands were quick and steady. He gathered plants on sunny days and on moonlit nights. Some he crushed, others he dried, still others he pressed for their juice. He combined them in secret proportions to make medicines that could cure aches and pains, soothe sore throats and comfort tired eyes and stomachs that hurt from eating too much. He gave away his lotions and potions to any creature that needed them. He watched his children play and was truly happy.

Far away from Jambavan, another story was unfolding. For a long time, the Sun had owned a dazzling jewel called Syamantaka. It was so bright that it even eclipsed the light of the Sun himself. One day, he decided to give this magnificent jewel to a man named Shatrajit, who worshipped the Sun every day, as a reward for his devotion and loyalty.

The jewel was not only bright but anyone who possessed it would be protected from harm. The jewel produced bags and bags of gold each day and if a king owned it, his lands would be rich and prosperous and safe from enemies. Shatrajit was overwhelmed by the jewel and though he loved it dearly, he decided that he should give it to his brother, Prasenajit, who was the ruler of a province on the western shore. Prasenajit was thrilled with the gift and wore it around his neck all the time.

One day, Prasenajit went hunting and got separated from his companions. As he went deeper and deeper into the dark woods, the jewel shining on his chest, he was attacked and killed by a lion. Even the lion could not resist the jewel and took it away, carrying it in his mouth.

Meanwhile, Jambavan sensed all was not well in his kingdom – his keen nose could smell blood and his alert eyes and ears told him that the animals had been disturbed by something. Jambavan left his cave and entered the forest. Before long, he saw the lion who had stolen the Syamantaka. Jambavan felt that a jewel so exceptional could only cause more and more trouble and so he gathered all his remarkable strength and attacked the lion, killing him with one swipe of his massive paw. Jambavan picked up the jewel and when he got home, he gave it to his children to play with.

When it became clear that Prasenajit and the jewel had both disappeared, Krishna, the prince of Dwaraka, became concerned. He set off to find out what had happened. In the deep forest, he found Prasenajit and his horse. He noticed bloody paw prints leading away from the lifeless bodies and followed them only to find a dead lion and another set of paw prints leading still further away. Krishna did not stop and those paw prints led him to a clearing in the forest.

On one side was a cave and in front of it, in the dappled sunlight, he saw children playing. They were tossing a bright, shining object to each other, laughing if it fell to the ground. Krishna realized this was the Syamantaka jewel that he was seeking. As he was about to take it away from the children, a great shadow fell over him. He looked up and saw a gigantic bear, his teeth bared, his claws out, ready to defend the children and their toy.

For twenty-eight long days and twenty-eight long nights, Krishna and Jambavan fought each other. Slowly, Jambavan began to tire. 'How can this be happening to me?' he wondered. 'I am the mightiest creature in all the three worlds. No one is stronger than me, no one has more energy, no one is a greater fighter.' When he could no longer stand, he sank to his knees in surrender. Krishna lifted him up gently and introduced himself. Jambavan realized he had been fighting the great god Vishnu who now lived in the world of men in the form of Krishna, prince of Dwaraka.

'I did not know it was you! I would not have fought so hard, if I had known,' said Jambavan. 'The jewel is yours, Krishna. Take it and do with it as you please in the world of kings and princes. Here in the forest, it is just a bright and shiny toy. Let us put this fight behind us, let there be no enmity between us. I give you my lovely daughter, Jambavati, as a wife. Treat her as you would the Syamantaka – she is as precious and much more valuable. She will light up your life as this jewel lights up everything around it.'

Krishna left the forest with two great treasures, Syamantaka and Jambavati. And Jambavan went back to making medicines that would relieve pain and discomfort.

8

Vali and Sugriva

Long ago, in the monkey kingdom of Kishkindha, Vali, son of Indra, the storm god, was king. He had the boon of absorbing half the strength of whomever he was fighting and while this made Vali a great warrior, it also made him arrogant. He had a quick temper and sometimes he acted in haste. But Vali was a good king – his kingdom was peaceful and prosperous, his people were happy. Vali lived an easy life in Kishkindha with his wife Tara, his son Angada and his younger brother, Sugriva, whose wife's name was Ruma.

While there were many who avoided combat with Vali because of his boon, there were others who were determined to test their might against the king of the monkeys. Ravana, lord of Lanka, had heard all about Vali and his great strength. And so, when he was on his campaign to defeat all the kings of the world, he arrived in Kishkindha with his army.

'Where is Vali?' Ravana asked loudly. 'Tell him to come out and fight me!'

Vali's ministers hurried out, trembling before the ten-headed rakshasa who was known to be invincible in battle. 'Vali has gone to the southern ocean to perform his daily worship,' they said. 'You can wait for him here.'

'I have no time to waste. I want to conquer him now and make him say in public that I am greater than he is! I will go to wherever he is and defeat him there in single combat.' Ravana instructed his army to stay where it was and wait for his return. He swiftly mounted his flying chariot Pushpaka, and made for the shores of the southern ocean.

He saw Vali, large and glowing like a mountain of gold, performing his rituals for the day. Ravana was struck by his splendour, but only for a moment. He decided to creep up behind the great monkey and grab him around the waist. But Vali knew that someone was about to strike and without interrupting his prayers, he used his powerful tail to tie up the rakshasa king with all his ten heads and twenty arms.

After he had finished his offerings, he turned to Ravana and said, 'My evening prayers are not done. You are my prisoner, you will have to come along with me as I travel to the other three oceans.' He tucked Ravana under his arm and rose into the air with ease.

From the south, he went to the eastern ocean, then the northern and finally, the western ocean, stopping at each to perform his rituals. Ravana was bound securely by Vali's tail and when they flew through the air, he dangled from under Vali's arm as if he were a child's toy.

Finally, they reached Kishkindha and Vali set the rakshasa on the ground. 'So, shall we fight?' he asked, laughing.

'I can see that you are strong and brave, perhaps you are stronger than me, even though I have ten heads and twenty arms. Why don't we make a pact of friendship instead?' said Ravana, holding on to all the dignity he could muster.

Vali clapped Ravana on his back, placed an arm about his shoulder and led him into Kishkindha. 'Stay here for a few days. Rest and restore yourself before you go off to find more kings to fight with!' The monkey and the rakshasa walked into the city, swearing eternal friendship.

All was calm in Kishkindha for a long time after Ravana left. Then, one day, Dundubhi, an asura who had the form of a buffalo arrived at the gates of the city, stamping his hooves, kicking up the dirt and tossing his head. He bellowed, 'Come out, Vali! Come, test your strength against mine! Even if you take half my strength, I know I can defeat you!'

Never one to turn down a challenge, Vali charged out of the city gates and attacked the buffalo. The fight was short and violent. Vali picked up Dundubhi by his horns and tail. He placed him across his knees and snapped him in half as if he were the branch of a tree. Roaring like thunder, he kicked the bloody and broken carcass of the buffalo which flew into the air for miles and miles, over the hills and valleys of Kishkindha.

Far away, on a quiet hilltop, the sage Matanga was meditating outside his hut. Dundubhi's body landed in front of him, spraying Matanga with blood and gore. The sage was enraged and shouted into the sky, 'Whoever you are, wherever you are, I curse you for splashing me with unclean blood. If you set foot on this mountain named Rishyamuka, your head will split into one thousand pieces!'

Vali heard those words coming out of the sky and laughed. 'I can stay away from one mountain if I have to!'

And once again, all returned to normal in the monkey kingdom. Not for long, though. This time, the asura Mayavi, Dundubhi's eldest son, banged on the city gates at night. 'Vali! I am younger and stronger and bigger than my father, Dundubhi! Leave the comfort of your warm bed and the soft arms of your wife – show me what you are worth!'

Vali crashed through the city gates with his brother, Sugriva, following close behind. Mayavi saw the two great monkeys coming towards him and took to his heels, charging over rocks and streams, his hooves not seeming to touch the ground. In the clouded moonlight, the brothers chased him as hard as they could. Suddenly, Mayavi seemed to disappear into the earth ahead of them. When they reached the spot, they saw a crevasse that led to an underground cave.

'Leave him, brother,' panted Sugriva. 'He'll stay underground for a while!'

Vali shook his head. 'I'm going in there and I'm going to kill him. You go back to Kishkindha and protect the city in case he finds a way out of the cave.'

'No, I'll wait here,' said Sugriva. 'In case you need help.'

Vali plunged into the darkness of the crevasse and Sugriva stood outside, every muscle alert, his heart beating like a thousand drums. For a long time, there was silence and then, Sugriva heard the sounds of a bloody fight – thuds and bumps and shrieks and screams and yells and roars. He couldn't tell which sounds came from Vali and which from Mayavi, so he stayed where he was, shaking with fear. Then he heard the most ghastly scream – it made his hair stand on end – and a gushing, foaming stream of warm blood came pouring out of the opening in the earth. Sugriva was sure that his brother had been killed, that this was his blood, that it had been Vali who was screaming. Sugriva pushed an enormous rock over the hole where the blood was coming from, hoping to trap Mayavi inside the earth. And he ran back to Kishkindha to tell Vali's people what had happened.

Vali's ministers listened gravely to Sugriva's story as Vali's wife, Tara, wept quietly, believing that her husband had been killed.

'Kishkindha needs a king, Sugriva,' said the ministers after they had conferred with each other. 'Angada is just a boy. You must take the throne in Vali's place. Let us arrange for your coronation without any delay.'

Sugriva protested a little but he knew the throne could not be left vacant, especially if monstrous Mayavi were to return. So he was crowned, but it was a sad city and there were no celebrations for the new king.

Sugriva ruled Kishkindha but the monkeys had not forgotten Vali and Sugriva knew that. He took his pleasures and let his ministers take care of everyday matters that came up.

All was quiet until one day, there was a huge commotion at the gate. Vali stood there, bruised and bloody, but as tall and strong as ever.

'Where is that brother of mine?' he roared. 'He left me to die so that he could take the kingdom and my wife! Do you know he rolled a huge stone over this hole in the earth so that I would be buried alive? Traitor! Tell him I have returned to reclaim what has always been mine!'

Vali smashed the city gates and stormed into the palace where he used to live. He strode into the inner apartments, he dragged his brother out into the courtyard and started to kick and pummel him without mercy.

Sugriva threw himself at Vali's feet and begged for a chance to speak. Tara, Vali's wife, ran over and held Vali back. 'Let him speak, Vali. Listen to what he has to say!' she cried.

Vali stepped back and wiped the sweat off his forehead. 'What do you have to say for yourself?' he growled.

Sugriva blubbered through his tears. 'Brother, I thought you were dead. I heard those screams and I saw that stream of fresh blood and I thought Mayavi had killed you. I closed the mouth of that hole because I wanted to trap Mayavi in the earth, not you! I swear this is true!'

'You had no faith in my strength!' shouted Vali. 'You betrayed me! You left me to die! But I'm going to kill you now!'

Tara and Ruma and all the ministers tried to calm Vali. They spoke softly and held his arms and stroked his broad back. 'He is your brother, your younger brother,' they said. 'He is like your child. He made a mistake, he doesn't deserve to die. Don't do something you will regret,' they pleaded.

The anger in Vali's eyes subsided and he relaxed a little. 'All right,' he said. 'I won't kill this idiot! Get up, look at me,' he said to Sugriva. 'I will not kill you. But I will send you away from Kishkindha. You are exiled from the land of your birth. If you set foot in this kingdom ever again, I will kill you. Now get out!' he said.

Knowing Vali's temper and fearing for his safety, Sugriva went with a few companions to live on the Rishyamuka mountain where, because of the sage Matanga's curse, he knew Vali could not come.

9

The Death of Vali

Sugriva felt safe on the Rishyamuka mountain where he lived with his six loyal companions. Years before, his brother Vali had been cursed by the sage Matanga to die if he were ever to set foot on the mountain.* And so it was that Vali could not go there and Sugriva could live in peace and without fear.

After he had exiled Sugriva from the kingdom, Vali was happy in the city of Kishkindha, enjoying the company of Tara and Ruma, eating sweet roots and fruits and drinking the honey liquor that the

---

*To read the story of why Vali was cursed, go to page 79.

monkeys loved. But Sugriva brooded about his brother and the injustice that had been done to him. He planned to get Kishkindha back, even if it meant getting rid of Vali once and for all.

One day, he looked down into the valley and noticed two men walking by the lake. Strangers never came to Kishkindha and Sugriva was curious about who they might be. It crossed his mind that they had been sent by Vali to kill him. So he asked his most loyal and bravest companion, Hanuman, to go and find out more.

Hanuman leapt from rock to rock as he made his way down the mountain. He approached the two men who walked tall and strong. Their chests were wide, their eyes were clear. They carried shining weapons but their hair was matted as if they were ascetics who lived in the forest.

'I am Hanuman. I am the companion of Sugriva, the great monkey. Who are you?' he asked as he bowed before them, for he had guessed that these were not ordinary men.

One of the men replied, 'I am Lakshmana and this is my brother, Rama, prince of Ayodhya. His wife was stolen away while we lived in the dark Dandaka forests. We are searching for her now –

we know she has been taken south, but we don't know who took her.'

'Come and meet Sugriva, my master,' said Hanuman. 'He will help you find your princess.' Hanuman lifted the men on to his shoulders and made his way up the mountain as easily as he had come down. He introduced the princes to Sugriva who welcomed them politely but without warmth.

Lakshmana explained how they had come to be in Kishkindha – Rama's exile, the kidnapping of Sita and the vulture Jatayu's dying words which had brought them to the monkey kingdom. As the great bird breathed his last, he had told the princes to seek out Sugriva as an ally. Then Rama asked for Sugriva's help to get his beloved wife back.

Sugriva listened carefully and then he said, 'Listen to my story, prince of Ayodhya. I too have lost my kingdom and my wife. My brother Vali took them both. Help me kill Vali and I will call together an army of monkeys such as you have never seen. They are strong and brave and they are as large as mountains. They fear nothing and nobody and they are the finest warriors in these lands. I will send them to the ends of the earth to find your wife. If you help me, I will help you!'

Sugriva told Rama in great detail all that Vali had done to him and asked the prince to kill his brother. With fire as the witness, Rama and Sugriva pledged to help each other. But Sugriva still had doubts. 'How do I know that you can kill Vali – he is the strongest creature I know! Show me your skills!' he said to Rama.

Rama did not reply. But from his quiver, he pulled out an arrow, slim and sure and true. Before Sugriva could even blink, Rama had strung his bow and loosed the arrow which sped silently through the air.

'So?' Sugriva asked. 'What have you done? I can't see anything. Who have you killed, what have you hit?'

Rama pointed into the distance. The arrow had pierced seven great sala trees that stood in a row, one next to the other, and noiselessly, it had come back to Rama's hand, as straight and sharp as when it left his bow.

Sugriva bowed before Rama. 'I'm sorry I did not have faith in you,' he said quietly. 'I know you will be able to kill Vali and get my kingdom back for me.'

The next day, the princes and the monkeys met

to decide how best to kill the monkey king. Rama said, 'Call your brother out of the city. Engage him in a fight, fight as hard as you can. He must not suspect anything. I will hide behind a tree and when Vali is focused on getting the better of you, I will shoot him. You have seen that my arrow is infallible.'

Sugriva agreed, though he was a little nervous that Rama might take too long to release his great arrows. Which meant that he, Sugriva, would get a good beating from his elder brother. Sugriva went to the gates of Kishkindha and though his legs were trembling, he managed to call out in a strong voice, 'Come out, Vali! Come out and fight me! You have taken my kingdom and my wife. I want them back!'

Vali was in the inner chambers, not quite awake. His servants came running to tell him that Sugriva was at the gates of the city and was challenging him to a fight. Vali laughed and rubbed his face. 'This won't take long,' he said to his own wife, Tara. 'I wonder what that fool is thinking – how can he have suddenly become strong enough to fight me? All he does is sit on that hill with his friends and brood.'

Vali strode to the ramparts and looked down at Sugriva. 'What's happening, little brother? Do you want me to beat you up again? Haven't learned your lesson, have you? Go away! I'm not in the mood to fight today.'

'Come out, Vali!' roared Sugriva. 'Or have you become too fat and lazy with all that good food you've been eating?'

Vali jumped down from the ramparts, his tail making an arc in the air behind him. The brothers started to punch and pummel each other, they scratched and bit each other, they slapped and kicked each other. They rolled on the ground and the dust rose around them, hiding them from view. When they were fighting, it was hard to tell whose legs were whose, which arms and which tail belonged to whom. Rama stood behind a tree, straining his eyes to tell the monkeys apart.

At some point, Sugriva pulled away and ran. His companions followed him with Rama and Lakshmana. They could hear Vali's mocking laughter in the distance as he turned and went back into the city.

Safe under the sheltering rocks of Rishyamuka, Sugriva burst out, 'Look at me! I'm bruised and bleeding!' he said to Rama. 'Why didn't you shoot Vali with your famous arrows that never miss their mark?' He turned away, muttering, 'What kind of friend is this? He obviously cannot protect me from Vali, I've made a terrible mistake!'

Rama spoke quietly and firmly. 'You and your brother look exactly alike, especially when you are covered in dust. I could not take the risk of shooting you instead of Vali. Ask for another fight . . .'

'You want me to get beaten up again?' shouted Sugriva as he wiped the blood from the wounds on his arm. 'What kind of ally are you?'

'This time, wear a garland of forest flowers so that I can identify you,' said Rama. 'Trust me, I will not let you down.'

'Do it quickly,' said Sugriva, still angry. 'I don't have the strength for a long fight after what Vali did to me today.'

The next morning, Sugriva placed a garland of wild flowers around his neck and went back to the gates of Kishkindha. He yelled for Vali to come out.

This time, Vali was not amused. 'I'll finish off that idiot today,' he said to himself. 'I've had enough of this irritation.' He stormed out of the gates, roaring loudly as he charged towards Sugriva. He went straight for his brother's throat, wanting to choke the life out of him.

Sugriva ducked and weaved, staying out of reach of Vali's vice-like arms. Again, they fought each other viciously, using their sharp claws and strong teeth as they punched and kicked. Flowers from Sugriva's garland fell like rain, but the garland stayed around his neck.

Suddenly, Vali lunged forward and fell to the earth, screaming. Sugriva saw that an arrow, with feathers that shone like gold in the morning sun. was sticking out of his brother's back. He collapsed on the ground, panting, but with a smile on his face. His trust in Rama had not been in vain.

However, he was soon overcome with sadness. He remembered the happy years of his childhood, when he and Vali had leaped and played together among the rocks and trees of beautiful Kishkindha, how Vali had always given him the sweetest fruit, taught him to swim in the river, carried him home when he was tired.

Sugriva crawled over to where his brother lay dying and stroked his mighty chest. 'How did it come to this, my brother?' He sighed as he took off his garland and tossed it away.

'It was my fault,' whispered Vali. 'I should not have treated you so badly. It was my duty to take care of you, not to bully you and exile you from the land of our fathers.' He winced in pain but continued to speak. 'Look after my son, Angada. Let him be king of the monkeys after you. Treat him like your own child, do for him all the things that I did not do for you.' Tears ran down Sugriva's face as he promised Vali that he would care for Angada.

Sugriva rose and collected himself. He called for his companions and said, 'We must prepare for Vali's funeral. We will mourn him for seven days and seven nights. Only then will I be crowned king of Kishkindha.' He turned to Rama and said, 'Thank you, my friend. You have fulfilled your part of our bargain. Come and live with us in our beautiful city. As soon as the rainy season ends, the mighty monkeys that I command will begin the search for your wife. Be our guest until then.'

Rama shook his head. 'I have sworn not to enter a city as long as I am in exile. Go, enjoy your kingdom and your kingship. I shall live in the caves around Kishkindha. When the rains end, Sugriva, I will remind you of your promise. Do not fail me!' he said as he embraced Sugriva in friendship.

Rama and Lakshmana walked away from the city while Sugriva took Angada by the hand and led his people through the gates of Kishkindha.

10

Hanuman Leaps for the Sun

There was a beautiful apsara named Punjikasthala who had emerged into the world during the churning of the ocean, along with the other lovely apsaras. They all lived in heaven where they were dancers in the court of Indra, king of the gods. One day, for some reason, Indra was displeased with Punjikasthala and he cursed her to take the form of a monkey and live on earth. Punjikasthala came to earth, where she was known as Anjana, and married the monkey Kesari. Every now and then, she would return to her celestial form and wander about, enjoying the time she had by herself and in her own familiar body.

Once, when she was walking alone on a mountaintop, Vayu, god of the wind, flew by and was immediately struck by her beauty. He stopped and said, 'Lovely lady, come with me! I will give you a mighty son who will have the form of a monkey. But he shall have my strength, my speed and all my other exceptional qualities. He will make you proud! He shall be praised and remembered in all the three worlds!' Anjana agreed and went with Vayu.

Soon after, a sweet, furry little monkey was born to her. Anjana cared for him and took him everywhere. But there was one occasion when the little monkey was asleep and so she left him on his own as she went down to the river to bathe. The monkey woke up and looked around. He was hungry, there was no food anywhere and worse still, he could not see his mother. He began to wail and then, he looked up at the sky. He saw the sun rising high, red and rich and ripe as a great big juicy fruit. Without hesitating for a moment, the monkey sprang upwards and flew higher and higher, chasing the sun to eat him.

Across the skies on the other side of the world, Rahu, the asura of the eclipse, was also chasing the sun. This was the day when he was allowed to swallow the sun for a few hours and appease his permanent hunger. Rahu was enraged when he saw another creature in the sky, apparently heading for the same food that he was. He ran to Indra and shouted, 'Indra, you gave the sun to me as my food. Now there is another Rahu who is chasing him and wants to eat him. Do something!'

Indra mounted his great elephant, Airavata, who was decorated with tiny golden bells that tinkled when he moved. Indra whipped out his thunderbolt and flung it towards the baby monkey who was getting closer and closer to the sun. The monkey grabbed the sun but when he saw Rahu, he thought the asura was another fruit and charged towards him. Rahu turned and fled. Just then, Indra's mighty thunderbolt struck the flying monkey who crashed to the earth. He fell on to a mountain and broke his jaw and lay on the rocks without moving.

Anjana was distraught when she found her injured child and wept loudly. Vayu came rushing to see what had happened and he, too, could not believe his son had been struck by Indra, king of the gods. He picked up his child and went off to

hide in a cave, refusing to blow in the three worlds.

When Vayu disappeared into the cave, there were no soft breezes to carry the fragrance of flowers from forests into the city, the wings of birds and bees and butterflies grew stiff, there were no dancing ripples in lakes or streams or rivers, leaves on trees fell still and silent, humans and other creatures found it difficult to breathe, their joints ached and they could barely move. There was no more laughter and the earth grew hot and dusty.

After a few days of this, living beings could not bear the situation any longer. They prayed to the gods and begged them for help. The gods, too, were suffering without the wind, as the smoke from the sacrifices and rituals could not be carried up to them in the heavens. They gathered and decided it was time to ask Grandfather Brahma for help. They went to him and bowed low and together, they cried, 'Dear Grandfather, help us! We are in great discomfort. Vayu has ceased to blow and living beings on earth and all the creatures of the three worlds are in pain. Please, tell Vayu to come out of his cave!'

Brahma went to Vayu and spoke to him gently. 'Why are you doing this, Vayu? The three worlds need you. Come out, blow again, let the worlds feel your soothing presence.' Vayu, who was holding his injured son in his lap, told Brahma that Indra had struck down his son with his thunderbolt and that he would only return to the three worlds when his son was well and strong again. Brahma gently persuaded Vayu to accompany him to Indra's court. All the gods followed them, hoping for the best.

'What have you done, Indra?' said Brahma. 'Vayu is upset because of your thoughtless action. We have to make this up to him. Let us give boons to Vayu's son, who already has his father's power and speed, that will make him the most powerful monkey ever!' Brahma leaned forward and touched the monkey with his hand, which was as soft and beautiful as a lotus petal. The little monkey opened his eyes and began to shine like a small sun in his father's arms. At once, the wind began to blow and all the creatures in the three worlds sighed with relief.

Indra was embarrassed and wanted to be the first one to protect the monkey. He said, 'This monkey will be known in the three worlds as Hanuman because he fell and broke his jaw. I give him protection from my thunderbolt. No one will be able to defeat him in battle!'

One by one, the other gods came forward and blessed the little monkey with boons and good wishes. The Sun gave him part of his own energy and brightness and promised that he would grow up to be learned and wise. Varuna gave him long life, safety from water and protection from his noose for one hundred years. Yama gave him freedom from sickness and the power to remain tireless in battle. Kubera protected him from maces and battle clubs, Shiva made him invulnerable to all his weapons. Pleased with what they had done, the gods went back to where they had come from. Vayu took Hanuman to Anjana and told her all about the boons.

~

Hanuman grew strong and fearless. He followed the Sun from the mountains where he rose to the mountains where he set, and learned the seven grammars from him, thus becoming a great grammarian. But because Hanuman was a monkey, he was also quite mischievous. He ran off whenever he wanted and went wherever he pleased. He jumped from tree to tree, stripping off their leaves and branches. He picked ripe fruit and ate it all by himself. Sometimes he hid and threw rotting fruit at those who passed by. But his favourite mischief was to harass the sages and wise men as they meditated and performed the sacred rituals.

Nothing gave Hanuman greater pleasure than breaking the clay pots which held the purified water for the rituals, or tearing up the sages' clothes of bark, or running off with the sacred kusha grass and other materials gathered for the rituals, or throwing things into the fire on the sacrificial altar, or distracting the wise men with whoops and swoops as they tried to concentrate.

The sages knew that he was protected from various weapons and also by the blessings he had received from the gods when he was an infant. There was little they could do to stop him as he was lithe and quick and could always put himself out of reach in the higher branches of trees. And so, the sages complained to Anjana. But despite being scolded by all three of his parents – Anjana, Vayu and Kesari – the little monkey kept up his pranks.

Finally, the sages had had as much as they could take. Even though they knew that expressing anger would set them back in their sacred and ritual practice, they cursed the monkey. 'Hanuman! You have tormented us with your strength and your swiftness and all your other special powers. You have not listened when we asked you to stop obstructing us in duties and in our work. Because of this, we curse you to be confused, to forget all your powers, to forget all that you have learned. You will live as an ordinary monkey, with other monkeys like yourself.'

And so it was that Hanuman grew into an adult monkey not knowing who he really was and not remembering all that he could do.

11

Hanuman's Adventures

Hanuman went about his life as a grown-up monkey, unaware of his powers because of the sages' curse. One day, Rama and Lakshmana, the princes of Ayodhya, arrived in Kishkindha in search of Rama's abducted wife. Sugriva, who lived in exile on the Rishyamuka mountain with a few loyal companions, sent Hanuman to find out who these men were and what they wanted. When they met face to face, Sugriva and Rama realized that they were in very similar situations – they were both princes in exile and their wives had been taken away from them. Rama and Sugriva made a pact of friendship – Rama would help Sugriva regain his kingdom and Sugriva would call together the great monkeys of Kishkindha and send them to the four corners of the earth to find Rama's beloved wife.

When the search for Sita began, Hanuman led a band of heroic monkey warriors into the unknown lands of the south. After travelling through forests and mountains and deserts, the monkeys reached the shore of the ocean and were stunned by what they saw – great sheets of water that rose and fell, roaring and thundering as they seemed to reach for the sky before they crashed on the rocks. Sparkling fish and other slithery water creatures that the monkeys had never seen before twisted and swam in the waves, catching the sunlight on their fins and scales as they were tossed about in the restless waters.

Sampati, a wingless vulture, who had been stranded on that shore years before, told the monkeys that he had seen a woman in great distress being carried in an aerial chariot by Ravana, lord of Lanka, to his island fortress in the middle of the ocean. She had to be Sita, Rama's wife. If the monkeys could cross the waters to the island, they would be sure to find her.

The mighty monkeys, all proud of their ability to leap great distances, began to brag and boast about how they might reach the island that was so far away. Only Hanuman sat in silence until Jambavan,* the wise old bear who had accompanied the monkeys on their southern travels, spoke up. 'It's you, Hanuman, you are the one who can cross the ocean in a single bound. You are the son of Vayu, the wind god. You have his speed and his strength. Let me remind you who you are and what you can do.' And then, with all the other monkeys present, Jambavan told Hanuman about his childhood, his boons and special powers and the curse of forgetting that the sages had placed on him.

Hanuman listened to everything the old bear had to say and shook himself as if he were waking from a deep sleep. With a loud cry that echoed through the air, he leapt to the top of Mount Mahendra. He took a deep breath and began to expand – his chest puffed out, the muscles on his

* See the story 'Jambavan, King of the Bears' on page 69.

arms and legs began to bulge, his eyes opened wide and seemed to spit fire, his magnificent tail curled above his head like a battle banner. The earth groaned as Hanuman pushed down on the mountain with all his strength, shattering it to pieces. The monkey pushed his arms in front of him as if he was parting the clouds and in a moment he was airborne: faster and higher than he had ever been, higher and faster even than when he had leapt for the sun as a baby.

Hanuman ripped through the clouds and tore through the sky on his way to Lanka. Mount Mainaka rose from the depths of the ocean so that Hanuman could rest on his summit, but the monkey touched him gently in thanks and kept on his way. The rakshasi Surasa tried to stop him by holding on to his shadow but he dove into her stomach and ploughed through her entrails, leaving her a lifeless heap on the ocean floor. Simhika, another rakshasi, tried to eat him because of the boon she had received from Brahma but he made himself as a small as a fly and flew in and out of her mouth before she could close her massive, hungry jaws around him. When Hanuman reached Lanka and landed on the sandy shores of the island, not a hair on his head had been harmed, nor was he even slightly out of breath.

Moving stealthily in the shadows, Hanuman entered that dark, glowering city, avoiding the bright light of the full moon. He crept silently through Ravana's palace which had pillars of gold and silver, windows of crystal and was scattered with soft couches covered in brocades and silks. He smelled the rich foods and fine wines that lay on tables that groaned under their weight and he saw women who were more beautiful than the full moon which was shining in the sky that night. He stopped and stared for one awestruck moment at the majestic ten-headed lord of the rakshasas who snored gently as he slept, but he knew he had to find Sita quickly.

Hanuman searched for Sita everywhere until he stumbled upon a grove of ashoka trees where, among the hideous misshapen rakshasis, he saw a sad and lonely woman whose beauty was like that of the moon hidden by clouds. 'This has to be Sita,' he thought to himself. 'She is the only unhappy woman on this island.' He reduced himself to the size of a cat and quickly climbed into the tree above her. Silently, he dropped Rama's ring onto

the grass where she would see it. Sita looked up in fright when she saw the ring, but Hanuman sang to her quietly about Rama's adventures, his troubles and his heartache at being separated from her. He assured Sita that Rama would soon rescue her and kill the rakshasa king who had taken her away from him, from her family and from the world she knew and loved. Sita sighed and wiped her eyes and thanked the monkey for his kind words and the solace he had offered her. She urged him to hurry back to Rama and tell him how she couldn't live much longer without him. Hanuman bowed to her and left the grove as quietly as he had entered it. As he prepared to return to the northern shore of the ocean, Hanuman decided that he could not go back to the monkeys before he had seen the entire city of Lanka and noted its fortifications and its armoury. He needed to know what weapons the rakshasas had and where they were stored, where the gates to the city were and how they were guarded, who the warriors were and who the generals that led them into battle. He also wanted to see Ravana again, so that he could tell Rama and the others what they could expect from the enemy.

Hanuman increased in size as he left Sita and ran through the city, roaring and shouting as he knocked over towers with his fists and feet. He picked up rakshasa guards and tossed them over the ramparts into the sea. He did everything he could to get noticed and finally, when Ravana's soldiers attacked him, he allowed himself to be captured and taken before Ravana, bound from head to toe.

'I am Rama's messenger,' said Hanuman when he saw the mighty king of the rakshasas in his court, surrounded by his advisers and ministers. Ravana's ten heads, crowned with gold and jewels, and strong arms scarred with battle wounds, did not frighten Hanuman. He spoke calmly. 'Your death is near, Ravana! Mark my words!'

Ravana blinked his twenty eyes in amazement. 'A monkey? A monkey is going to be the cause of my death? This is outrageous! Who is this creature? Set his tail on fire and get him out of my sight at once!' he shouted as he gathered his silken robes, the colour of blood, around him and flounced out of his court.

The rakshasa guards gleefully poured oil on Hanuman's tail and set fire to it before they released the ropes that tied him up. In a trice, Hanuman had escaped his captors and could be seen running through the city setting it aflame. He climbed the walls and the ramparts, the towers and the gates, he ran through the narrow streets and the quarters where rakshasas lived with their wives and children. When the city was blazing, Hanuman heaved a great sigh and doused his flaming tail in the salt waters that surrounded the island. Without stopping to rest, he took off into the sky to return to the monkeys with all the information he had gathered.

~

Before long, Rama and his monkey army had reached the shores of Lanka by building a bridge over the turbulent ocean and were ready to take on the rakshasas for the sake of Sita. When the fighting began, Hanuman carried Rama on his shoulders into battle. Hanuman was everywhere – he used his nails and his teeth, his fists and his feet, he hurled rocks and stones and uprooted trees and turned them into deadly weapons. All his boons of safety from weapons and all his powers kept him free from harm as he crushed and smashed and slapped and kicked and punched and bit and tore at the rakshasas.

Even though the monkeys seemed to be winning, the rakshasas had better weapons and many tricks up their sleeves. They could use magic as well. Suddenly, Lakshmana was struck by the arrows of Indrajit, Ravana's son, and he collapsed to the ground. All the monkeys gathered around, wailing and screaming, terrified that Lakshmana was dead. Slowly, Jambavan the bear limped over. He held the fallen warrior's wrist and counted his pulse, he pulled up his eyelids and looked at his eyes. 'He is not dead,' he said to the others. 'But he could die very soon. There is only one thing that can save him.'

Jambavan turned and looked at Hanuman. 'On the slopes of the Dronagiri mountain, which is further away even than the mountains where the sun rises, there is a magic herb called the sanjeevani. If you can bring it here before the night is over, we can save Lakshmana. Go, Hanuman! Fly as fast as you can, every moment counts!' Even before the old bear had finished speaking, Hanuman had slapped his tail on the ground and risen upwards into the darkening skies.

Meanwhile, Ravana's spies had listened to Jambavan's words and they hurried to tell Ravana that Lakshmana could be saved. Ravana called for Kalanemi, a fearsome rakshasa whom he trusted completely, and said, 'Stop that monkey! I don't care what you do, but make sure he does not return before sunrise. Delay him on his journey! Kill him if you have to!'

Kalanemi had the power to change his shape at will and he could also make illusions that seemed real. He sped across the ocean and created a small island that was covered with trees and flowers and dotted with lakes of clear water. He disguised himself as a pious ascetic and sat down in front of his false hut, waiting for Hanuman.

Hanuman was tired and thirsty – the journey was long and he had been fighting all day. He looked down from the sky and noticed that delightful island which seemed so calm and peaceful. He landed in front of Kalanemi, who immediately welcomed him and offered him food and water. He pointed to the lake and told

Hanuman to refresh himself. Hanuman plunged into the cool waters, not knowing that hidden deep within them was a huge, hungry crocodile. The crocodile grabbed Hanuman by the leg and tried to drag him under the surface but Hanuman exerted his enormous strength, pulled the crocodile out of the water and smashed its head on the rocks.

At once, a beautiful apsara emerged from the crocodile's body and thanked Hanuman for ending her curse. She whispered to Hanuman not to trust the ascetic, that he was a rakshasa in disguise. Hanuman leapt over to where Kalanemi sat, pretending to say his prayers. The monkey grabbed the false ascetic by the waist, twirled him above his head as if he were an empty cloth bag and flung him across the waters in the direction of Lanka. Kalanemi landed at Ravana's feet in his rakshasa form, smashed like a rotten fruit that had fallen from a tree.

Hanuman rushed onwards, looking for the mountain that lay beyond the rising sun. As he got there, he noticed a faint light in the sky – the short night would soon be over. He realized he had no time to look for the precious herb that Jambavan needed to restore Lakshmana to life and health. For a moment he panicked and then, quick as a flash, he grew to his enormous size once more. He broke off the top of the mountain and soared into the air, carefully balancing the mountain peak on the palm of his hand, so as not to disturb the trees and plants. He summoned the speed and strength of his father, the Wind, because he had to reach Lanka before the goddess of the Dawn painted her eastern skies in streaks of red and gold.

Hanuman flew faster than lightning and thundered towards Lanka where the monkeys were waiting anxiously. They heard the great commotion in the sky and began to clap and shout, sure that Hanuman was on his way back and that he had been successful. Even before he touched the ground, Hanuman lowered the peak gently on to the field where Lakshmana lay in his deathlike trance. Jambavan's assistant, Sushena, ran forward to pluck the life-giving herbs from the peak because he knew Jambavan was too slow to get to them before the sun rose. Tripping over himself as he ran, he brought the leaves over to the bear who crushed them in his great paws, muttering spells and incantations over them as he rubbed them under Lakshmana's nose.

Lakshmana's eyelids fluttered, his chest heaved. He coughed and opened his eyes. 'Have I overslept? Why are you all here? Come on, we have a war to win!' he shouted as he leapt up and grabbed his bow and arrows. The monkeys cheered and followed him into battle. Quietly, Rama bowed to Jambavan and touched the bear's tired, dusty old feet.

~

After days of fighting, Lakshmana managed to kill Indrajit, Ravana's eldest and most beloved son. As the funeral pyres for Indrajit, who had once defeated the king of the gods, and for so many other heroic rakshasa warriors blazed, and the women of Lanka wailed and beat their breasts for their fallen husbands and brothers and sons and fathers, Ravana knew he needed help. He called for Mahiravana, his half-brother, who ruled Patala, the underworld. 'Help me, brother. This is for the pride of our family. Take Rama and Lakshmana away, kill them in the underworld. Destroy the morale of this ridiculous army of monkeys. The rakshasas cannot be defeated by forest dwellers who have no weapons except trees and rocks!'

Mahiravana took on the form of Vibhishana, Ravana's brother who had become a trusted ally of the monkeys. In that form, he fooled Hanuman into letting him into the tent where the princes slept and he whisked them away to his kingdom under the earth. When Hanuman was told what had happened he was deeply ashamed and vowed to bring the brothers back safely without any help. 'I know my brother Mahiravana,' said Vibhishana. 'He will sacrifice the princes to the bloodthirsty goddess Chandi, he is her devotee. Hurry, Hanuman, hurry!'

Hanuman began to dig a tunnel in the ground, tossing mud and sand and rocks in all directions with his powerful arms and legs. He went deeper and deeper till he disappeared from view. Inside the dark earth, Hanuman eventually came to a lighted doorway. He was about to break down the door when he was stopped by a very strange creature who seemed to be half-monkey and half-reptile.

'I am Hanuman. Move aside, please, I don't want to hurt you. Who are you, anyway?' said Hanuman politely, even though he knew time was running out.

'Look at me,' said the creature. 'I am Makaradhwaja, I am your son!'

'I have no son,' said Hanuman. 'I don't even have a wife and I don't spend time with women.'

'Dear Father, I have been waiting to meet you for so long,' said Makaradhwaja and he tried to embrace the mighty monkey that stood before him. 'I was born when a crocodile swallowed a drop of your sweat as you flew over the sea!'

'Very well, then,' said Hanuman. 'Since you are my son, you must help me rescue the princes of Ayodhya whom your master has kidnapped. Tell me, how can I kill Mahiravana, lord of Patala.'

'I have heard,' Makaradhwaja whispered, looking around in fear, 'that Mahiravana's life is held within the flames of five different lamps. All of them have to be blown out at the same time for him to die. I think all the lamps are in this room which I am guarding.'

'Just do as I say,' said Hanuman confidently.

Hanuman and Makaradhwaja pretended

to have a huge fight, shouting and yelling and pushing each other and stamping their feet. Hanuman knocked Makaradhwaja out and stormed into the inner room where Mahiravana was lolling on his couch surrounded by beautiful women. At a glance, Hanuman saw there were five lamps in five different directions, impossible to extinguish with a single breath. There was only one way he could take Mahiravana's life. He transformed himself into a five-headed creature with the heads of a boar, an eagle, a lion, a horse and his own monkey head. All five heads pulled in all the breath they had and forced it out in a great gust. The five lamps were blown out, the room darkened and Mahiravana fell from his throne, dead.

Hanuman revived Makaradhwaja and with his help, located Rama and Lakshmana. He brought them to the surface of the earth, still fast asleep. This time, the monkeys did not clap and cheer when they saw Hanuman emerging from within the earth as they did not want to wake the sleeping princes. But they whispered among themselves and smiled broadly as Vibhishana put his arms around Hanuman in a warm embrace.

The very next day, Rama killed Ravana in battle and the war was over. The monkey army had defeated the mighty rakshasa forces, Sita had been rescued and it was time for Rama to go back to Ayodhya and reclaim his kingdom after fourteen long years in exile. In the spirit of celebration, Rama invited the leaders of the monkeys and bears and the rakshasa Vibhishana to come back with him so that they could enjoy the festivities around his coronation. They all climbed into Pushpaka, the flying chariot that had belonged to Ravana, and accompanied Rama back to his home.

Because Hanuman was as swift as the wind, he went ahead to prepare Ayodhya for Rama's arrival. Rama's brothers, Bharata and Shatrughna, made all the preparations for the coronation and the citizens of Ayodhya danced and sang and decorated their city with colourful buntings and flowers. The dust on the streets was tamped down with fragrant water, flags flew from the tops of buildings and oil lamps glowed in every window. Rama's coronation was attended by everyone, rich and poor, young and old. Rama gave his friends and allies rich presents of gold and jewels as he bade them farewell and thanked them for all they had done to help him.

When it was Hanuman's turn to say goodbye, Rama's eyes filled with tears. He held the great monkey close and took off a necklace of pearls that he had been wearing. He placed it around Hanuman's wide shoulders and the monkey shone like a moon garlanded with stars. 'Hanuman, my dearest friend,' Rama said. 'You found my wife, you saved my brother's life and mine. I can never repay you for that. But I promise you this – you shall live as long as my story is told on earth. The three worlds will know you and praise you and remember you forever. Whenever anyone thinks of me, they will think of you. Go in peace, great monkey.'

Hanuman bowed and left Rama's presence.

12

When Bhima Met His Brother

After Yudhishthira had lost his kingdom in the dice game against his cousins, the five Pandava brothers and their wife Draupadi had to spend thirteen years in the forest. They made the best that they could of their changed circumstances, but proud Draupadi suffered in their period of exile. She was unhappy with their simple lives, their ordinary food and their uncomfortable living quarters. She was ashamed of what her husbands had to endure, living like poor ascetics when they were, in fact, royal princes. But she continued with her duties as a wife and as a woman with a household to care for. She performed the daily rituals and worshipped the gods every day, asking for their grace and protection.

Once, when she was walking back from the shores of the river after her morning prayers to the Sun, a sweet breeze blew by and left a beautiful flower at her feet, a flower unlike any she had seen before. A heavenly perfume arose from the flower, making Draupadi giddy with delight. She buried her face in the delicate blossom, inhaling the sweet scent and caressing its petals which were softer and finer even than the silks she had worn in the palace. She ran to Bhima and cried, 'Look, Bhima! Have you ever seen a flower like this? Do you know what it's called? Can you get me some more?'

Mighty Bhima, strongest and most powerful of the Pandavas, knew that the flower grew and flourished far away, in the enchanted gardens of Kubera, which were guarded by heroic yakshas who were always ready for battle. He loved Draupadi with a gentle tenderness and would do anything to make her happy, so he replied, 'Ah, the saugandhika flower, I've never seen one before, but I've heard about them and I know where they grow. Of course, I'll bring you the flower. I'll bring you more than one. I'll bring you so many that you can make garlands and bracelets and anklets for your feet. You can place them in your hair and still have some left over.'

Bhima was the son of Vayu, the wind god, and could travel over great distances with ease. He knew that only he would be able to bring the flowers back for Draupadi and so he set off in a northerly direction, tracking his path by the sun which shone brightly above. He carried his mace with him, in case he encountered hostile creatures or forest dwellers, for the region was full of unknown dangers. With great determination, he walked and climbed, trusting his instincts about how to reach the shaded groves where the flowers could be found.

The sun crossed its zenith in the sky and began its downward journey towards the horizon. Bhima felt a change in the air and a moment later, his nose was filled with the perfume of the saugandhika blossoms. 'I must be close to where they grow,' he

said to himself. 'I can only imagine what it must be like to smell hundreds of them at the same time!' he thought and quickened his pace.

He moved through the trees until suddenly, he was stopped by what seemed like a thick rope stretched across the path. 'What is this?' he thought irritably to himself. Bhima looked around and saw a grizzled old monkey, asleep by the side of the path. The rope that lay before him was the monkey's tail. Bhima went up to the monkey and shook him. He shouted rudely, 'Hey you! Get out of my way. Move your tail!'

The monkey slowly opened one of his yellow eyes and yawned. He said, sleepily, 'Why are you shouting?'

'I am shouting because you are in my way and because you seem quite deaf. Move your silly old tail so I can go onward!'

'Ah,' said the monkey. 'Won't you tell me who you are and where you are going? This is not a safe place for humans.'

'It's none of your business who I am and where I am going,' replied Bhima, full of impatience. 'But let me tell you that I am Bhima, second of the five Pandava brothers. My father is Vayu, the wind god! I am mighty and strong, no one stops me from getting what I want!'

'Son of Vayu, eh?' said the old monkey with a smile.

'Yes, I am the son of Vayu. I am the brother of Hanuman, the great monkey who was Rama's dearest friend, the monkey who found Sita, the monkey who set fire to Lanka. My brother is a fearless warrior and he helped Rama win the war against the rakshasas!'

'Hanuman?' said the monkey. 'Am I supposed to know who that is?'

'What kind of monkey are you?' said Bhima, 'How can you not know Hanuman who is the mightiest of all the monkeys in the world? He is so strong that he can carry a mountain on the palm of his hand. He flies through the air, he's as swift as our father, the Wind. Rama loves him so much he has given him the gift of eternal life! Surely, you know about Hanuman!'

'I forget a lot of things these days.' The monkey sighed. 'Anyway, tell me where you're going.'

Bhima felt a little kinder towards the old monkey and said, 'I'm going to Kubera's garden to fetch some saugandhika flowers for my wife.'

'That's a place not open to mortals,' said the monkey. 'But you seem like a strong young fellow, so you should try your luck. If you don't want to step over my tail, just pick it up and move it aside. I'm tired and all this requires effort. I'm going back to sleep.'

Bhima stepped forward to move the monkey's tail off the path. He tried to lift it. The tail was heavy, really heavy. He pushed, he shoved, he kicked against it with his feet, he pushed his mace under it to heave it aside, all to no avail. He sweated and strained, he groaned and he grunted, but he could not move the tail one single inch. Finally, he gave up and collapsed on the ground, panting. It struck him that this was no ordinary monkey and he should show him some respect. He reached out and touched the old monkey gently. 'I'm sorry. Tell me who you are and allow me to pass.'

The monkey looked Bhima in the eye. 'Don't you know me, brother?'

Bhima fell backwards in surprise. 'Hanuman! You are Hanuman! How could I be so stupid and not see that?' He hugged the monkey close, patting his back and stroking his head, laughing and crying at the same time. Hanuman held him tight and Bhima felt a new strength and power course through his veins. 'Stay with me, brother,' he said to Hanuman. 'Let me have your strength and your wisdom all the time.'

'I'll come to you when you need me, Bhima,' said Hanuman. 'All you have to do is call. I know you are heading into a terrible war with your cousins. I will protect you and your family. I will appear on Arjuna's battle banner as the promise of your eventual victory. Go now, go find the flowers for your wife.'

Bhima bowed to the great monkey and said, 'Please, can I ask you for something before I leave?'

'Of course,' said Hanuman.

'Just for one moment, show me your gigantic form, the one you took when you leapt over the ocean to find Sita,' begged Bhima.

Hanuman smiled and began to expand. His chest puffed out, his limbs grew long and firm and pulsed with muscles, his magnificent tail arched proudly over his head. He grew beyond the tallest tree and seemed higher than any mountain Bhima had ever seen. He seemed to touch the sky as clouds settled on his enormous chest, looking like garlands of white lotuses. Bhima could not get enough of this wondrous sight and as he was about to faint in wonder, Hanuman was back by his side along the path, his tail curled around him. He stroked Bhima's cheek with his furry paw and bade him farewell.

Bhima went onwards and soon he entered a clearing in the forest that was filled with flowering plants and vines. Pools of clear water sparkled in the dappled light that came through the trees. Bhima inhaled the gentle fragrances of this sacred grove. He lay on the soft grass and closed his eyes – he could see his beloved Draupadi's smiling face.

All at once, the grove was filled with fierce yakshas. With their weapons raised, they fell upon Bhima, shouting, 'We are the guardians of this garden which is loved by Kubera, our master. No humans are allowed to enter here!'

Bhima rose and shrugged off the yakshas as if they were mosquitoes. He swung his huge mace in the air and brought it crashing down on them, injuring many with that single blow. He pummelled others with his feet and fists, he picked them up by the dozen and flung them through the air. Some of them got stuck in the low hanging branches of trees, others landed heavily on the ground, bruised and battered. The band of yakshas scattered in all directions. They picked up their injured companions and limped away, blood and tears streaming down their faces.

Kubera, the lord of wealth, heard about the commotion in his garden and came there to see who had disturbed his peaceful realm. 'I am Bhima Pandava, the son of the Wind. Mighty Hanuman is my brother,' roared Bhima when he saw Kubera. 'I will destroy this place if you come any closer to me!'

'What do you want here? Ask me and I will give it to you with pleasure,' said Kubera, smiling. 'There's no need for any more destruction.'

Bhima calmed down and bowed to Kubera. 'Lord,' he said, 'I have come here to collect these saugandhika flowers for my wife. We are living through troubled times and they will make her happy for a little while.'

'Take as many as you like, Pandava. Take them as a gift from me to your wife. When she braids them in her hair, she will know that she has my blessings!'

Bhima thanked Kubera and carefully gathered

only the flowers that had fallen to the ground. His journey home seemed to take no time at all and when he got there, he showered Draupadi with the fragrant blossoms. His heart overflowed with joy when she smiled and thanked him.

13

Vritra Swallows Indra

Tvashtri lived in the heavens and was the artisan of the gods – he made beautiful things for them, including their weapons. Long ago, Tvashtri created a mighty son and because he had given him three heads, he named him Trishiras. The three heads were monstrous, but Trishiras was a great ascetic. He had controlled his senses and was capable of performing austerities that no one else could – not the sages, not the gods, not even the asuras.

When Indra learned that Trishiras was amassing great powers through many difficult penances, he became afraid. 'He better not replace me,' he thought to himself and started to make plans to destroy Trishiras's concentration. He went to the beautiful apsaras, the dancing girls in his court, and said, 'Go and dance in front of Trishiras. Take his mind off his austerities. Distract him so that he has to start all over again, from the beginning. Do not let him gain the powers he needs to defeat me and take my place as king of the gods!'

The apsaras quite enjoyed tormenting meditating ascetics and had often been successful in destroying their hard work of years. They got dressed in their finest clothes, they lined their eyes with kohl and coloured their lips with the juice of berries. They rubbed their bodies with sweet-smelling oils and perfumes, they wove celestial flowers into their hair and tied little bells on their ankles. But all their swaying and singing and calling and dancing did nothing. Trishiras remained unmoved. The apsaras returned to Indra and admitted their failure. 'Oh never mind,' said Indra angrily. 'I'll think of something else!' and he dismissed them.

Then it occurred to Indra that he could use his great thunderbolt, made from the bones of the sage Dadhichi, to slay Trishiras. He hurled his mighty bolt with all his strength and the three-headed ascetic fell to the ground. But even after he was dead, his body radiated so much heat and energy that Indra was blinded and scorched. As he was running away, he found a simple forest dweller and said to him, 'Please cut off those three heads! I will send all my powers and the power of my thunderbolt into your axe. But do this, do this now!' The forest dweller swung his axe at Trishiras and as his heads fell to the ground, sparrows and partridges and quails emerged from them and filled the world. Indra was relieved of his torment and he and the forest dweller went their separate ways.

By killing Tvashtri's son, Indra had killed a brahmin, a terrible act that would come back to haunt him. A year later, the great gods Vishnu, Shiva and Brahma came together and confronted Indra. Indra had to undergo severe penances and purification rituals to make up for what he had done, he even had to perform the great horse sacrifice. But eventually, he became worthy of being the king of the gods again.

Meanwhile, Tvashtri heard about the death of his son and was enraged. He vowed to create an

even mightier son who would destroy Indra. He poured ghee and other powerful liquids into the sacred fire. A huge creature emerged, so large that he enveloped the skies and covered the sun. 'Vritra, my son!' roared Tvashtri. 'Kill Indra!'

Vritra set to his task with great enthusiasm. He attacked Indra vigorously and the two fought each other many times. Once, Vritra even swallowed Indra and the other gods had to make him yawn so that Indra could slip out of his mouth. Yawns have been a part of our lives on earth since then.

Indra and Vritra fought for days and for nights. They fought for weeks and for months. They would take breaks every now and then, but their duels would resume as ferociously as before. It seemed as if Indra would never defeat Vritra. Finally, the gods gathered and went to Vritra. They said to him, 'Our king cannot defeat you and you cannot defeat him either. You have filled the entire universe. The sky is dark and you hold back the waters of the rivers. Can you not live in friendship with Indra?'

Vritra smiled and said, 'Yes, I can. But you must promise me that the gods will not kill me. They must not attack me with something that is wet or that is dry, something that is made of stone or of wood, neither by a thunderbolt nor by a weapon and neither during the day nor the night.' The gods agreed and went away happily.

But Indra was seething with rage. He was jealous and afraid, he knew he had to kill Vritra if he was ever going to be safe again. One evening, as the sun was setting, he saw Vritra alone on the shore of the ocean. He remembered the conditions that the gods had agreed upon and thought to himself, 'It is twilight, so it is neither night nor day. I can put all my powers into the foam on the waves – that is neither wet nor dry. Nor is it a weapon.' Indra drew all his energies together and sent them into the foam which he directed at Vritra. When the foam struck him, a fever unleashed by the great god Shiva entered Vritra. What it did to him was terrible and the gods stood by and watched in fear and wonder. Vritra's mouth blazed with fire and a ghastly jackal emerged from it. Flaming meteors rained around him and vultures and other birds wheeled around his head, shrieking and crying out in hideous voices.

When Vritra collapsed and died, the skies cleared, a sweet breeze blew and all creatures in the three worlds sighed with relief. They clapped and shouted and sang songs of praise. But there was one more thing and no one was prepared for that. Out of Vritra's body came a horrifying woman. She had huge teeth and staring eyes, her hair was wild, she was as skinny as a skeleton, she wore a necklace of skulls and she was smeared with blood from head to toe. All beings trembled when they saw her and quickly covered their eyes. They knew she had come for Indra, that she was the punishment for what he had done.

Indra had run away after he killed Vritra and the three worlds suffered in his absence. The earth turned dry and barren, rivers changed course, lakes disappeared. All creatures were afflicted but none more so than Indra himself. He was restless, he was feverish, he wasn't comfortable in his own body. He knew that the ghosts of the brahmins he had killed, Trishiras and Vritra, had come to haunt him. He ran here and there, from one end of the three worlds to the other. But nowhere could he find the peace he sought. Finally, he hid himself inside the stalk of a lotus that bloomed in a faraway lake and stayed there, quaking.

But the horrifying woman searched every corner of the three worlds and found him inside the lotus stalk. She grabbed him around the neck and instantly, Indra was paralysed.

Brahma, grandfather of the gods, realized what had happened and begged the woman to give Indra up. She smiled, baring her sharp teeth, and said, 'I will return him to you. But where will I live? You must find a place for me to be, for I cannot go back to where I came from.'

Brahma thought for a while and then he called the trees and the plants and the herbs and the grass and said to them, 'Take a part of this hideous creature and let her live in you. I promise that she will do you no harm.'

But the trees and plants and herbs and grass trembled and pleaded, 'Lord, please do not give her to us permanently. We are already so weak – we bear the wind and the rain and the drought, and people cut us and break us. Let someone else share this burden.'

Brahma said, 'Whoever cuts you and breaks you on the first day of the moon or on the day of the full moon or after sunset will be afflicted by this creature too. Now go in peace.'

Then, Brahma called the waters to him, the streams and the river and the lakes, and asked them to take the rest of the horrifying woman. The waters agreed but like the trees and the plants, they asked that someone else take a share too. Brahma said, 'The people who do not respect the waters, who pollute them with excrement and waste matter, they will suffer for what they have done.' And the waters agreed and went away.

At last, Indra was free. He went back to rule the kingdom of heaven as before.

14

The Cursed Immortal

Ashwatthama was born to live forever. He had a jewel embedded in his forehead, a gift from the great god Shiva because of the severe penance that Ashwatthama's father had performed for a mighty son. The jewel prevented him from feeling hunger, thirst and fatigue in battle and it gave him power over all forms of life that were lower than human. Ashwatthama was born to the brahmin Drona and his wife Kripi when they were very poor. Drona was unable to make enough money to look after his family so, sometimes, he would feed his child flour mixed with water. Ashwatthama would drink the liquid eagerly, thinking it was milk.

When things became even more desperate, Drona decided to visit his old friend Drupada, who was now the ruler of a prosperous kingdom, and ask him for help. But Drupada scorned him, refusing to remember the friendship they had shared as young boys at the hermitage of sage Bharadvaja. 'Only equals can be friends, Drona,' scoffed the king. 'If you ask for alms as a poor brahmin would, I might help you, but we are no longer friends. Look at me, I am a king. And you are a beggar!' Drona felt deeply humiliated and poison entered his heart. He swore that he would take revenge on Drupada as his equal, as a warrior.

Drona rejected his brahmin occupation and found work through his wife's brother, Kripa, at the court of the Kauravas. There he trained the young princes in the arts of war and became the most respected and formidable teacher of weapons in the whole world. His son, Ashwatthama, grew up with the princes, never quite their equal, but always their friend. His father taught him all he knew about fighting and weapons, just as he taught the royal princes and, in their shadow, Ashwatthama grew into an invincible warrior.

As the distance between the one hundred

Kaurava boys and the five Pandava boys grew wider and their disputes over land and kingship grew more fierce, Ashwatthama chose to be loyal to Duryodhana, the eldest Kaurava prince. He knew his father, Drona, favoured the Pandava, Arjuna, but Ashwatthama felt obliged to the family that had employed his father and given him dignity and a livelihood.

Eventually, a brutal war between the Kaurava and Pandava cousins erupted. It lasted eighteen long days and millions of men and animals and all kinds of creatures were mercilessly slaughtered. The earth turned red, slushy with spilled blood, the sky grew dark with circling vultures, and jackals and hyenas howled with impatience to get to the corpses that rotted on the battlefield.

On the fifteenth day of the war, Drona killed his old friend Drupada in a sword fight. The Pandavas knew that Drona could only be killed if he laid down his weapons. And so, advised by Krishna, they decided to deceive him. An elephant named Ashwatthama was killed and they shouted, 'Ashwatthama is dead!' Knowing that the eldest Pandava, Yudhishthira, would never lie, Drona asked him, 'Is this true?' Yudhishthira muttered,

'Ashwatthama, the elephant, is dead!' Drona heard only part of his words and believing that it was his son that had been killed, he put down his arms. Drupada's son, Dhrishtadyumna, born from the sacrificial fire, emerged from the shadows and cut off Drona's head.

Ashwatthama was inconsolable at the death of his father and vowed to take revenge on the Pandavas who had killed their teacher with trickery. Blinded by tears, Ashwatthama unleashed one of the great weapons he had inherited from his father. The Narayanastra tore through the Pandava forces and many were killed. But not enough to end the war.

As the battles raged on, Ashwatthama watched his friends and his allies and the princes he served with love and loyalty die one after the other. Some were killed fairly in battle, others were slain in dishonourable ways, none more so than Duryodhana, killed by Bhima who, on Krishna's secret signal, smashed his mace on Duryodhana's thighs. As Duryodhana lay dying, he appointed Ashwatthama commander-in-chief of what was left of the Kaurava army.

That night, Ashwatthama was exhausted and

he was wounded. Along with his uncle, Kripa, and the general, Kritavarma, he hid in a dense forest, trying to decide what he should do next. The other two warriors fell asleep, but Ashwatthama spent a sleepless night, wondering how to destroy the Pandavas. As he fretted and fumed, he stared at an enormous banyan tree that was filled with scraggly nests in which crows and their young were fast asleep. A flash of light caught the corner of Ashwatthama's eye and when he turned his head, he saw a huge owl, its white wings more silent than thought, alighting on the tree. The owl's eyes shone golden, its beak was sharp and its gleaming talons were ferocious. Even before Ashwatthama could admire the bird's majestic beauty, it uttered a blood-curdling screech and attacked the sleeping crows. In a storm of blood and feathers, the owl killed the crows and their sleeping children. The ground under the tree was littered with half-eaten bird bodies, wounded and terrified babies, shattered eggs and destroyed nests. The owl retired to a distant branch and wiped its beak and talons clean.

Ashwatthama took this as an omen, a sign for what he needed to do. He would attack the

Pandava camp as it slept, he would kill the Pandava children – that was the only way to avenge Drona and Duryodhana and all the others who had been killed in this war that had lost all meaning.

Quickly, he woke his companions. 'Come,' he said to them. 'We must attack the Pandava camp now, while they are asleep. We can kill them all!'

'That's against the rules of war,' stuttered Kripa as he rubbed the sleep from his eyes.

'Nothing about this war has been honourable, no one has fought by the rules. My own father was killed by a lie! Our king was felled by an illegal blow to his thigh!' shouted Ashwatthama. 'This is our chance to end the war. It is a chance at victory for our side! Come with me. Please!'

Kripa and Kritavarma strapped on their weapons and followed Ashwatthama. They crept towards the Pandava camp where everything was silent. 'Guard the exits,' whispered Ashwatthama. 'I will attack the front.' He moved through the shadows, silent as the owl's wings and came to the entrance. Ashwatthama's weapons glinted in the light of the dying torches as he leapt towards the gate.

In complete silence, he slaughtered the guards

as they slept but, as he prepared to enter the camp, he was stopped in his tracks. There in front of him stood Shiva Bhairava, god of destruction. Blood dripped from the weapons he carried in his many arms, his eyes blazed with fire, the serpent around his neck stood rampant. He was surrounded by ganas, the aggressive troops who fought for him with no mercy. 'Fight me, Ashwatthama, if you want to pass. I am the one who gave you your jewel, your boons in battle!' hissed the great god.

Ashwatthama did not blink and attacked Shiva as if he was an ordinary soldier. He fought without fatigue and without doubt, he used every tactic he knew and every weapon he had, he fought as if he was possessed by the madness of war itself. It pleased Shiva and he blessed Ashwatthama. 'Go, child! Do what you must. I am with you.'

Ashwatthama tore into the camp where the sons and grandsons of the Pandavas and their allies and relations slept. His first target was Dhrishtadyumna, the man who had killed his father. He picked him up and broke his body in half, leaving him to bleed to death on the ground. He sought out the courageous warriors and commanders, killing them as if they were flies at a summer picnic. His anger unleashed and blessed by Shiva, Ashwatthama swept through the camp, slashing, cutting, smashing, crushing. If anyone escaped his onslaught, Kripa and Kritavarma slew them at the exits of the camp. Those who saw him believed he had taken on the form of Bhairava himself. Ashwatthama did not even spare the young warriors and the children, cutting their tender throats as one would harvest ripe wheat in the field.

In the blood-drenched morning after, Arjuna and Krishna and the other older Pandavas howled with rage when they saw the aftermath of the massacres. They chased Ashwatthama, swearing to kill him before the sun reached its zenith at noon. Ashwatthama had one weapon left, the Brahmastra which, if used, signalled the end of Time. In desperation, he picked up a blade of grass and empowered it with the magic that drove the deadly missile.

On the other side, Arjuna did the same. But the great sage Vyasa realized that when the two missiles clashed, it would be the end of the world. His voice rang out across the skies and he commanded both warriors to recall their missiles.

Arjuna obeyed, reluctantly. But Ashwatthama had not learnt from his father how to call back the weapon that would destroy everything. He had released it, set it free, all he could do now was to change its direction.

Ashwatthama, outsider to everything – to power and glory and love and redemption – powered the Brahmastra into the womb of Abhimanyu's widow, Uttara. She was pregnant with mighty Arjuna's grandson but when the Brahmastra found its target, the last descendant of the Pandavas was killed. The royal lineage of Hastinapura had come to an end.

The raging sorrow of the Pandavas led them to revenge. Ashwatthama, broken and defeated in spirit by all that he had seen and done, was captured and the Pandavas demanded that he surrender the wondrous jewel in his forehead. Krishna, cousin to the Pandavas, cursed Ashwatthama – the open wound on his forehead, from where the precious jewel had been snatched, would ooze blood and pus forever. He could not die. Ashwatthama would live in constant pain, he would stink of death and decay and be shunned by humans who would treat him like a rabid dog. All doors, all kindness would be closed to him and he would wander homeless and rejected throughout the worlds, through endless Time.

15

Trishanku's Heaven

There was a king called Trishanku who was virtuous and also very handsome. He was learned and often had long conversations with wise men and teachers about the big questions of life – what does it mean to be good, what are the rewards for good action, what is heaven – these were some of the ideas that Trishanku turned round and round in his mind and discussed with his teachers. After all that he had heard about good deeds and the realm of the gods, he decided that he wanted to go to heaven while he was still alive. He believed he would go to heaven anyway, since he performed all his duties as a king: he took care of his people, his kingdom was peaceful and prosperous, he was loved by his wives and children.

So he went to his teacher, the sage Vasishtha, and said, 'Sir, I am a good man, I know that I will attain heaven when I die. I want to go there now, while I am alive, as I am, in my human body. Is there some secret ritual, some magic spell, some potion that I can drink that will take me there? Surely you know a way to make this possible.'

Vasishtha frowned. He was not pleased. 'Your majesty, this is not possible. No one can go to heaven in their human body. Only the soul, which survives after death, can make that journey. This is what the gods have decreed and it has been the case forever. Please put this idea out of your mind. Heaven will wait for you.'

Trishanku was not discouraged by his teacher's words. He was sure he would find someone to help him get to heaven as he was. First, he approached Vasishtha's sons, all teachers in their own right, but not yet as skilled or as respected as their famous father. 'Your father says he cannot send me to heaven in the body that I now have,' said

Trishanku. 'Perhaps you can help me – maybe you know things that your father does not.'

Vasishtha's sons were enraged and they scolded the king. 'How dare you!' they shouted together. 'How can you ask us for something that our father has already refused? He has given you the right answer – it is not possible to ascend to heaven in your human form! Do you think we know more than him? He is the greatest sage on earth! You have insulted him by coming to us.'

Trishanku was embarrassed but Vasishtha's sons were not done. 'You are vain, Trishanku. You take pride in your good looks. That's why you want to go to heaven in your human body. You think you will rival the gods. We will make sure that never happens!' They cursed Trishanku to become old and feeble and in an instant, Trishanku had turned into an old man, wearing smelly, ragged clothes, covered in dust and dirt. Trishanku was shocked and he hurried back to his palace, but no one could recognize him and his ministers and retainers threw him out on to the street.

Helpless and hungry, Trishanku made his way to the hermitage of the other great sage,

Vishwamitra, who had become Vasishtha's rival ever since Vishwamitra had tried to take the divine cow, Kamadhenu,* away from Vasishtha. Vishwamitra was always looking for ways to thwart Vasishtha's plans and to make things difficult for those who held the gentle sage in high regard. He saw Trishanku's ragged figure coming towards him and at once, with his divine eye, he searched the king's past and saw all that had happened.

'Welcome,' he said to Trishanku. 'You seem hungry and tired. Come and rest here and have a meal. I have looked into your heart and I know why you are here. So what if Vasishtha was not able to do what you asked? I am far greater than him. I have powers that I have gained through my penance. I know what rituals and sacrifices we need to perform to take you to heaven in your human body! Recover your spirits and I will help you achieve your heart's desire.'

'I am a king, I don't look like this or wear these clothes,' stammered Trishanku. 'I was handsome, I was clever, I am a good man. I did everything

---

*Read the story of Kamadhenu on page 33.

that I had to do. I honoured the sages and the teachers, I studied the sacred books, I performed the prescribed rituals, I walked the path of righteousness. I looked after my people and my kingdom. I know that I deserve heaven!'

'I know you do,' said Vishwamitra. 'Have no fear. I will call all the great sages and priests together and we will perform the rituals that will take you to heaven.' Vishwamitra summoned his sons and instructed them to send out invitations to all the learned sages in the land. Vasishtha and his sons were also invited to this grand occasion, when Vishwamitra would put his great powers on display. But they refused to come and so Vishwamitra cursed Vasishtha's sons – that they would be burned to ashes immediately and that they would be born one hundred times more, each time in disfigured and deformed bodies.

The day of the great ritual dawned and all the sages and priests gathered around the fire altar. Even though some of them were anxious about what they were trying to do for Trishanku, which was against the will of the gods, they were too afraid of Vishwamitra's anger to protest. Vishwamitra himself muttered the secret incantations and prayers while the others poured oblations into the fire as they recited the hymns that praised the gods and persuaded them to accept what was being offered.

But the gods did not come to the ritual, they stayed away. Vishwamitra got more and more angry and spoke the spells and incantations louder and louder. He grabbed the oblation spoon and began to pour ghee and other liquids into the flames himself. Still, there was no sign of the gods.

Vishwamitra turned to Trishanku. 'You can see that the gods are not responding. But I can send you to heaven in your human form in an instant with the power that I have gained through my austerities. Are you ready?'

Before Trishanku could say yes or even nod his head, he began to rise into the sky. All the sages, along with Vishwamitra's sons, were wonder-struck and watched with their mouths open as Trishanku rose higher and higher till he seemed about to pierce through the bright clouds behind which lay the realm of the gods.

Trishanku reached heaven and the gods, led by Indra, came forward. They said, 'You have to go back to earth, Trishanku. You cannot enter here in your human body, it is not allowed. Besides, you have been cursed. Go back, go back!'

At once, Trishanku fell back, his head pointing towards the earth and began to hurtle downwards. As the sages watched in horror, Vishwamitra shouted, 'Stop! Stop!' and Trishanku's headlong descent was suddenly halted. He was stuck in mid-air. The gods and Vishwamitra both asserted their powers at the same time and, as one pushed Trishanku upwards, the others pushed him down. King Trishanku was stranded, hanging upside down, between heaven and earth, neither here nor there.

Vishwamitra roared in anger, 'I know why this has happened. The gods will not allow Trishanku to enter heaven in this form. Never mind! I will create another heaven for him, a parallel universe. He will live in his human body in the new heaven that I make for him. My promise to him will not be in vain. Never let it be said that Vishwamitra did not keep his word!'

Immediately, Vishwamitra set about creating another universe, just like the one in which we live. He began with the stars and the constellations, picking the Seven Rishis first. They twinkled and shone as Vishwamitra created a copy of heaven in the sky. He was about to create another Indra to be king in this heaven, but the gods came to him and said, 'What are you doing, Vishwamitra? Have you lost your head? This is not what you gained your powers for. You cannot create the gods! Think before you act further!'

Vishwamitra stopped. His anger had faded and he realized what he was about to do was wrong and that it would destroy all that he had obtained through his practice of austerities. He sighed and shook his head. 'I promised Trishanku that he would enter heaven in his human body. I cannot go back on that. Let him live in this heaven I have just created. Let the stars and constellations that I have already made also remain. This, I ask of you.'

'Very well,' said the gods. 'But we must also respect Indra's wishes. Because of Indra, Trishanku hangs upside down between sky and earth. Trishanku can live in this heaven, but he will live upside down.'

Vishwamitra agreed, the great sacrifice was closed, the sages went back to where they had come from and Trishanku stayed in the heaven that had been given to him.

16

Prahlada and the Magic Cloak

In the eternal conflict between the gods and the asuras over who will rule the three worlds, sometimes the gods win and at other times the asuras are in control. Once there was a very powerful asura king called Hiranyakashipu – a long and complicated name that simply meant he had a cushion made of gold. If we wanted to, we could call this asura 'Golden Cushion'. Hiranyakashipu was angry a lot of the time because his older brother, Hiranyaksha (his name meant 'Golden Eyes') had been killed by the great god Vishnu. Hiranyakashipu had become king in his place and though he enjoyed the power and the glory of kingship, he was consumed by the desire to avenge his brother's death. And he was also angry that his young son, Prahlada, worshipped Vishnu with complete and unswerving devotion.

'Don't you know that I am the most powerful creature in the three worlds?' he roared. 'You should be worshipping me! All my subjects do, and even the gods quake in terror when they hear my name. How dare you place Vishnu above me! Look, I am right here, in front of you. See my powerful arms and my strong legs! Where is this Vishnu of yours? How do you know that he even exists?'

Prahlada smiled and said nothing as he turned away from his father and went back to his prayers and rituals. Hiranyakashipu tried many arguments to persuade his son to give up his worship, he tried bribes and gifts and other gentle persuasions and then he resorted to bullying and punishment. But the boy remained aloof, uninterested in his father's treats and equally indifferent to his threats.

Hiranyakashipu had a sister named Holika and like many asuras, she had magical powers and magical objects. One such magical object was a cloak that protected her from fire. When she wore it, she could walk through the fiercest flames without being harmed, without even feeling the heat. Hiranyakashipu decided to enlist her in his plans against Prahlada. He went to her and said, 'My son is getting out of hand. We need to teach him a lesson. I will prove to him that this Vishnu he worships is not all-powerful and cannot always protect him. I will announce a grand purification ceremony and light a huge fire in the city square. You must sit in the midst of the flames with Prahlada on your lap. You will be wearing your magic cloak so you will be safe and Prahlada will learn not to go against the wishes of his father.'

'What if he is burned to death?' asked Holika.

'Good riddance, then, if his precious Vishnu can't protect him!' replied Hiranyakashipu as he stormed out of his sister's room.

The news went out into the city about the ceremony and crowds gathered in the square to watch as a huge fire was built around Holika and Prahlada. Some people whispered, 'Poor child. How can a father do this?' Others spoke more loudly, saying, 'This will teach that boy a lesson.

Imagine worshipping your father's enemy!' The flames climbed higher and higher and smoke from the fire reached the heavens.

Great gusts of wind howled around the city and began to fan the flames. One of those gusts caught hold of Holika's magic cloak, tore it off her body and threw it over Prahlada, covering him completely as he sat calmly within the flames. Holika was no longer protected and as she died with a ghastly shriek the flames subsided.

The people rushed to Prahlada and when they saw him unharmed in every way, they praised him over and over again. 'The god he worships must have saved him,' they said to one another. 'Maybe Vishnu is even more powerful than our king!'

After this, Hiranyakashipu came to the conclusion that he would have to gain some extraordinary powers in order to confront Vishnu and so he embarked on a fearsome programme of austerities to achieve his goal. Finally, in response to the asura's determination, Brahma, grandfather of the gods, appeared before Hiranyakashipu. 'Ask for a boon, my child,' said Brahma. 'You deserve it.'

'I want to be even more powerful than I already

am,' replied the asura. 'I want to be beyond death, I want to be immortal!'

'Even I am not immortal,' said Brahma wistfully. 'I die when this cycle of Time comes to an end. And then, I am reborn along with the new world. You cannot have freedom from death. Ask for something else.'

'Well, then,' said Hiranyakashipu, 'I shall make myself impossible to kill. Give me the boon that I shall not be killed in the day nor in the night, not inside nor outside, by neither man nor beast, by neither a slashing weapon nor a throwing one, neither on land nor in the sky.'

'All those conditions will be met, you shall have these boons. But Death comes to us all, my son. We don't know when or where or how. May you live long and live happily,' said Brahma as he reluctantly blessed the asura and went back to his own realm.

Hiranyakashipu returned to ruling his kingdom, secure in the knowledge that he was as close to immortal as any creature could hope to be. He considered himself equal to the gods now and so he was outraged when he saw that his son still chose to worship Vishnu. 'Where is this Vishnu of yours? How come he never comes to see you or shows himself to anyone?'

'He is everywhere, all the time, Father,' said Prahlada. 'He is wherever you want him to be.'

'Everywhere? All the time?' shouted Hiranyakashipu. 'What does that mean? Prove it to me! Is he even in this solid stone pillar that holds up the doorway to my palace, this pillar that has stood here from the time of my forefathers?' The asura king kicked the pillar that was next to him. With a sound like a crashing thunder, the pillar split open and a wondrous creature emerged, half-man and half-lion.

This was Narasimha. He had the body of a man but with the fierce face and sharp teeth and flowing mane of a lion as well as a lion's sharp claws and great strength. Hiranyakashipu fell backwards in horror and in a trice, Narasimha grabbed him by his waist.

Narasimha roared and the palace walls shook. As the sun set and turned the sky a bloody red, he placed the asura across his knees and standing at the threshold of the palace, the lion used his sharp, wicked claws to tear open Hiranyakashipu's stomach. He dragged out his intestines, steaming and bloody, and tossed them onto the ground.

Writhing and screaming in agony, Hiranyakashipu died a horrible, violent death at the hands of a creature who was neither human nor animal. Held across Narasimha's lap, which was between earth and sky, Hiranyakashipu was killed at the entrance to the palace, in a place that was neither inside nor outside. He was torn apart by a lion's claws which were neither a slashing nor a throwing weapon, at twilight, a time that was neither day nor night.

As soon as the asura died, there was a great shouting and clapping from the heavens. All the gods had gathered in the sky to watch Narasimha, who was, of course, Vishnu, put an end to arrogant Hiranyakashipu.

But Narasimha's blood was up and he could not manage the anger and violence that he contained within himself. He rampaged across the city, wreaking destruction in all directions. People cowered in their homes. They hid under their beds and pulled their children away from the windows. No one was able to control Narasimha or calm him down. Even the gods feared what he might do next. Finally, one of them suggested that they send gentle Lakshmi, Vishnu's wife, to soothe the beast.

Lakshmi, born from the lotus, came to earth and stood before the man-lion. She placed herself on his left and gradually, Narasimha became calmer. Lakshmi sat on his lap and at last, his anger was cooled.

Vishnu appeared in his benign form and blessed Prahlada, who stood before him with his palms joined and his head bowed. 'You have been my brave and constant devotee. I will always protect those who love me and worship me,' he said as he placed his hand, which was as soft and beautiful as a lotus petal, on the boy's head. Then, in a flash of light, he vanished from the earth and rejoined the other gods in heaven.

Prahlada became king in his father's place and the gods and all creatures in the three worlds heaved a huge sigh of relief.

17

The Wondrous Story of King Ila

There was a king named Ila and he lived in the kingdom of Bahlika. He was beloved of his people and he was a good and just ruler. The gods and the beings of the air, the earth and the sky – gandharvas, siddhas, nagas, pannagas and yakshas – all worshipped him. All was well in the three worlds.

Spring arrived in Bahlika and Ila decided to go on a hunt to the forest with his courtiers and retainers. Along with his men, the king killed thousands and thousands of animals, but he was not satisfied. He went deeper and deeper into the thick forest, chasing down more and more animals, shooting them with his deadly arrows that always found their mark.

Suddenly, Ila found himself in the place where Kartikeya, the commander of the gods' armies, had been born. His parents, Shiva and Parvati, were enjoying themselves in that beautiful woodland and Shiva had turned himself into a woman to amuse his beloved wife. As Ila came closer, he saw that all the animals in the grove – snakes and birds and everything else – had also become females. He was surprised, but that was nothing compared to what he felt when he realized that he himself and all his companions had also been turned into women.

Ila saw the beautiful goddess Parvati standing near a waterfall and he begged her, 'Great goddess, what has happened to me? How have I become a woman? What did I do? How can I be a man again? I am a king, my people rely on me for their welfare!'

The goddess smiled when she saw the king's distress. She said, 'Since Shiva has already turned you into a woman, I can't change that. But my boon will make sure that you are a woman for one month and a man for the next month. When you are a man, you will forget that you were a woman. And when you are a woman, you will not remember that you were ever a man.'

'Please,' said Ila, 'may I be the most beautiful woman in the world when I am a woman?'

'Of course,' said Parvati.

In the first month that he was a woman, Ila wandered through the beautiful groves that were filled with lotus lakes and visited by many different kinds of birds. His companions had also become women and together they enjoyed the shady trees, the sweet fruit and the cool waters deep inside the forest. One day, Ila came upon a man, Budha, whose face shone like the full moon. He was immersed in a lake where he was practising severe austerities – he held his breath and remained underwater for hours, never moving, his eyes wide open, watching the fish and the other water creatures as they swam past him.

Through the water, Budha saw Ila, the most beautiful woman in the world, and his concentration was broken. He moved in the water and broke through the surface of the lake. 'Who can this woman be?' he wondered. 'She is even

more beautiful than the celestial dancers in Indra's court!' He walked towards his hermitage and when he got there, he saw four women. They were Ila's companions and Budha asked them about the woman he had seen. 'Does she have a husband, who is her father, to whom does she belong? Where does she come from and why is she here?'

'She is our mistress,' they replied, smiling sweetly. 'She has come here with us to enjoy the forest.'

Budha was confused and decided to go into a trance and use his special vision to see the truth. In a moment, he had learned everything about King Ila. He came out of his trance and he said to Ila's companions, 'Go, lovely ladies. There are many wonders in these forests, including men who are like you, sometimes male and sometimes female. You can make friends with them. By my grace, you will never be hungry and you will always be safe.'

When Ila realized that she had been deserted by her companions, she was afraid but Budha came up to her and reassured her. 'I am in love with you, my lady. Give yourself to me and we will live happily in this forest with the birds and animals for company.' They stayed together, Budha and

Ila, and in what seemed like a moment, the first month of spring was over.

In the second month, Ila rose from his bed, a man. He was alone and when he went outside, he saw Budha, engaged in his ascetic practice, standing in the lake with his arms raised above his head. Ila approached Budha and said, 'Sir, I am lost. I came here to hunt with my royal companions and my servants, but they have all vanished. Where could they have gone?'

Budha understood that the king had lost his memory, so he said, 'Do not be afraid. Your men were all killed in a massive storm. You came here, tired and frightened, and fell asleep in my hut. You have nothing to fear. You can stay here as long as you like, eating roots and fruits, as I do.'

'I cannot stay here, I am a king,' replied Ila, very upset. 'I must go back to my kingdom. I cannot abandon my people and my many wives. Let me go back just once. I will place my son on the throne, he is a good man.'

Budha did not want to let Ila go. 'Stay here for a year,' he said. 'I will make sure that everything turns out in your best interest.' So Ila stayed with Budha. He was a woman for a month and enjoyed the pleasures of the forest and Budha's loving company. Every other month, he would become a man and worry about his duties as a king and the welfare of his people. One month, when he was a woman, Ila gave birth to a beautiful son and handed him over to Budha.

Soon, the year passed and although he was happier than he had ever been, Budha remembered that he had to keep his promise to Ila, to act in his best interest. Budha was the son of a great sage and so he called together all the sages who lived in the forest. They arrived one after another, in pairs and in threesomes. When they were all gathered, Budha spoke to them. He said, 'This is King Ila. He is son of Kardama. You all know what happened to him. Now we must act for his benefit.'

The sages consulted each other about what would be best for the king who was sometimes a woman and sometimes a man and they considered various options. Kardama, Ila's father, also came there and joined the discussions. Finally, he said, 'Only Shiva can undo what he has done. We need to make him happy, and there is only one way to do that. There is no sacrifice more dear to Shiva than the ashwamedha, the horse sacrifice. If we perform that in Ila's name, Shiva is sure to grant him what he wants. Who is the best person to collect the materials, who will make the fire altar, who will chant the prayers and the secret sayings?'

The sages divided these tasks among themselves and soon, the sacrifice was under way. When it was over, Shiva appeared. He was smiling and said, 'I am pleased. Tell me, what can I do for you?' The sages asked the great god to make Ila a man again. Shiva was happy to do so and after accepting the praises and thanks of all who were there, he disappeared. The sages returned to where they had come from and Ila was free to go back to Bahlika, his kingdom.

Ila's people and his wives and his sons were all delighted when he returned after all those months, for they had given up hope of ever seeing him again. The entire kingdom rejoiced and celebrated for many days and weeks. Soon Ila divided his kingdom among his sons, giving them equal lands and wealth. And then, having attended to all his duties and responsibilities on earth, he died peacefully and went to heaven.

18

Mahishasura and the Goddess

Diti, the mother of the asuras, was sad and angry that her sons were constantly being killed in their battles with the gods. Unable to bear this any longer, she spoke to her daughter. 'How can we stop Indra and the others from killing the asuras time after time? You must do something to prevent your brothers from being slaughtered.'

Diti's daughter bowed to her mother and set off immediately for the forest. She found a clearing and after making a circle of five fires, she sat in the middle and began her ascetic practice. Her penance was truly awe-inspiring, it shook the three worlds and even Indra's throne rattled and swayed, causing him much discomfort and some confusion.

Diti's daughter remained firm in her practice until one day, a sage came to her and said, 'You shall have your wish, my child. You shall have a mighty son who will challenge the gods for control over the three worlds. Let your son ask Brahma for the boons that he needs to become invincible, and they shall be granted to him. Now, please, stop this, so that the universe is restored to its usual patterns.'

Having got the blessing she sought, Diti's daughter transformed herself into a female buffalo and wandered through the streets of the asura kingdom. The king of the asuras saw her and knew that she had only taken on the outward form of an animal. He decided to marry her and when their son was born, half of him was like a man and the other half was like a buffalo. He could take either form, as he pleased. His parents lovingly named him Mahishasura, the buffalo demon. His mother told him of the sage's promise and as soon as Mahisha was old enough, he went off to practise austerities of his own so that the gods would have to give him what he asked for.

Like his mother, he was fierce in his penance. Eventually, Brahma came to him and said, 'Your austerities are impressive. Tell me, what do you want?'

'I want to be immortal. I want to be invincible in battle, no one should be able to kill me!'

Brahma smiled and said, 'Only the gods never die. You cannot be immortal. But you can make it difficult for others to kill you.'

Mahisha thought for a moment and said, 'All right. Give me the boon that I can only be killed by a woman. Women are weak. I know that even if I were to meet a woman in battle, I could easily overcome her. So this boon will make me immortal!'

'As you wish,' Brahma said and vanished.

After his father died, Mahisha became the king of the asuras. Vidyunmalin, the great asura general, came to Mahisha and honoured him. He said, 'Sire, once we were the kings in heaven and we ruled over the three worlds. The gods took our place unlawfully. Bring us back to power, you have

the boon you need to defeat the gods!' Mahisha knew that it was his turn now to declare war on the gods and so he gathered the asura armies and attacked the gods.

The gods sent their best and brightest warriors forward, they used their most formidable weapons and their most deadly battle formations, but they were no match for the asuras led by Mahisha. The great gods Vishnu and Shiva both entered the fray, but all their skills and all their powers and all their weapons were of no use. Indra was defeated and Mahisha took his throne. He occupied Indra's city, Amaravati, he rode Airavata, Indra's magnificent elephant, he commanded Indra's charioteer, Matali, he even danced with the apsaras. The asura had won a decisive victory and he ruled the three worlds.

Utterly dismayed, Indra led the gods to consult with Brahma, Vishnu and Shiva. 'We have no hope against this buffalo. He has taken everything we have. How will we restore ourselves to our rightful place in heaven? We are the gods, that's where we live. The asuras should occupy the underworld. How do we send them back there?' he said, his forehead wrinkled with worry.

'There is one last chance you have,' said Brahma. 'The boon this asura asked for and the boon I gave him was that he could only be killed by a woman. Combine your energies, gods of the earth and sky and fire and water! Combine your energies with those of Vishnu and Shiva and create a woman, a goddess, more powerful than each of you individually. She will defeat Mahishasura!'

Slowly, the gods released their energies that emerged as rays of light, as flashes that resembled lightning, as glittering threads, as blazing shafts. Vishnu and Shiva did the same and soon a glorious woman appeared before them. 'Give her your weapons!' shouted Brahma and as each god held out his weapon for her, the goddess produced an arm to take it from him. She took Indra's thunderbolt and Varuna's noose and Yama's staff and Agni's spear and Vayu's mace and Vishnu's discus and Shiva's trident and when she had a weapon in each of her eight arms, a great tawny lion appeared. She mounted the lion and smiling, she said to the gods, 'Have no fear. I will kill Mahisha for you!'

When the splendid, shining goddess roared, the earth shook. When she laughed wildly in excitement, eager for battle, and tossed her dark hair, the ocean shrank back from the shore. But the gods were not afraid. They raised their arms and praised the goddess, bowing low before her and touching their foreheads to the ground. They adorned her with jewels and decorated her with flowers and worshipped her.

On his throne in Indra's palace, Mahisha heard the uproar that rang through the three worlds. 'What is this? What is happening?' he bellowed like the buffalo that he was.

'Sire, the gods are regrouping. A new divine being has been created to defeat you,' said his courtiers.

'Come!' shouted Mahisha. 'The battle calls!' he said as he strapped on his armour and picked up his weapons. The asuras ran into battle cheering and shouting, convinced that their king would lead them to victory again.

They attacked with all their weapons – arrows and spears and lances and swords and clubs and battleaxes. The sky grew dark as missiles from both sides flew through the air. It rained arrows but the flashes in the darkness were not lightning, they were the glistening blades of sharp swords as they whistled through the air.

In the middle of the melee, the goddess blazed with energy – it seemed as if nothing and no one could touch her as she slashed and swung and pierced and hurled all the weapons at her command. Her face was serene as she struck the asuras down with her arrows, as she slashed them in half with her sword, as she caught them in her noose and bound them hand and foot, as she clubbed them to pulp with her mace, as she pinned and pushed them into the ground with her trident.

When Mahisha saw his army being crushed in this manner, he transformed himself into a massive buffalo and attacked the goddess's troops with his hooves and horns and tail, snorting and panting and pawing the ground. He gored some of her troops with his horns and others he tossed so that they fell to the ground in a heap, he pulverized them with his hooves, some he ensnared in his huge tail and with a flick, he threw them to a great distance, he made others unconscious with his hot breath. Then, maddened with his success, he attacked the goddess's lion, seeking to plunge his deadly horns into its belly.

The lion roared and reared up, the goddess raised her sword and shouted with delight, for she knew that now Mahishasura's moment of death had arrived. Laughing, her mouth red and showing her teeth which were like freshwater pearls, she slashed at the asura's body and cut it in half. As the buffalo's body thrashed and writhed on the ground, Mahisha emerged from it in the shape of a man. He gazed at the goddess, dazzled by her splendour and her beauty, blinded by her wild hair. But before he could ask for her mercy and grace, she plunged her trident into his neck. He died with his eyes open, shocked that he had been killed by a woman.

When Mahishasura fell, there was a great tumult. The asuras ran from the battlefield, shrieking and wailing, and they headed straight for the underworld where they would remain for aeons. At the same moment, the gods broke into cries of joy, shouting 'Victory! Victory!' and the goddess's triumphant laughter danced and echoed throughout the three worlds.

Note on the Author

Arshia Sattar has a PhD in classical Indian literatures from the University of Chicago. Her translations from Sanskrit, *The Ramayana of Valmiki* and *Tales from the Kathasaritsagara*, have been published as Penguin Classics. She has also written books for children, including the *Ramayana for Children*.

Note on the Illustrator

Ishan Trivedi began his career as a comics illustrator in 2009. His influences range from miniatures and patachitra to madhubani and kalamkari. He brings the sensibility of traditional Indian styles to digital illustrations. He especially likes illustrating mythology and fantasy, and enjoys doing work for children.

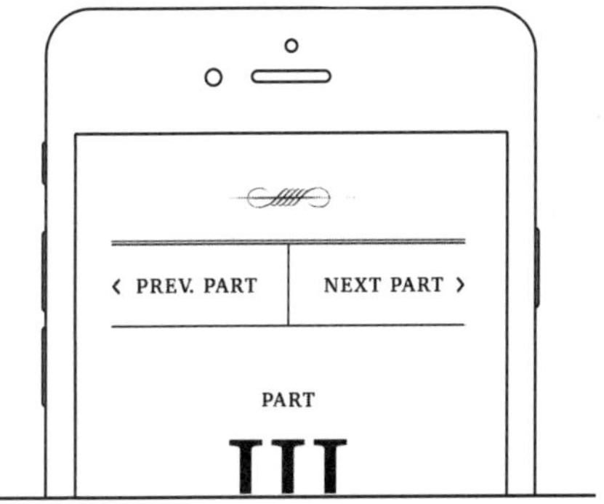

Beautiful Typography

The quality of print transferred to your mobile. Forget ugly PDFs.

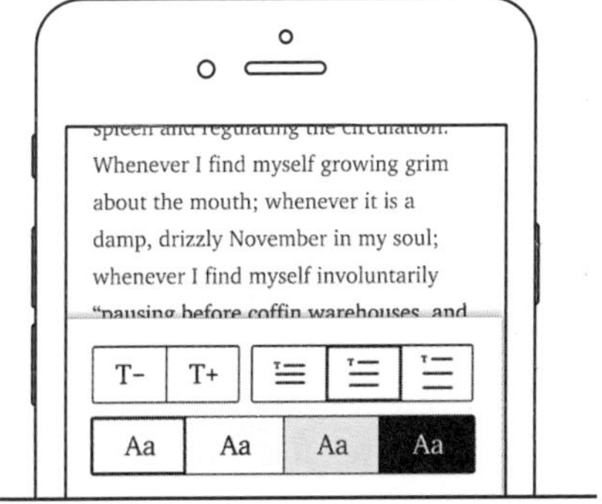

Customizable Reading

Read in the font size, spacing and background of your liking.

AN EXTENSIVE LIBRARY

Fresh new original Juggernaut books from the likes of Sunny Leone, Twinkle Khanna, Rujuta Diwekar, William Dalrymple, Pankaj Mishra, Arundhati Roy and lots more. Plus, books from partner publishers and all the free classics you want.

www.juggernaut.in

DON'T JUST READ; INTERACT

We're changing the reading experience from passive to active.

Ask authors questions

Get all your answers from the horse's mouth. Juggernaut authors actually reply to every question they can.

Rate and review

Let everyone know of your favourite reads or critique the finer points of a book – you will be heard in a community of like-minded readers.

Gift books to friends

For a book-lover, there's no nicer gift than a book personally picked. You can even do it anonymously if you like.

Enjoy new book formats

Discover serials released in parts over time, picture books including comics, and story-bundles at discounted rates.

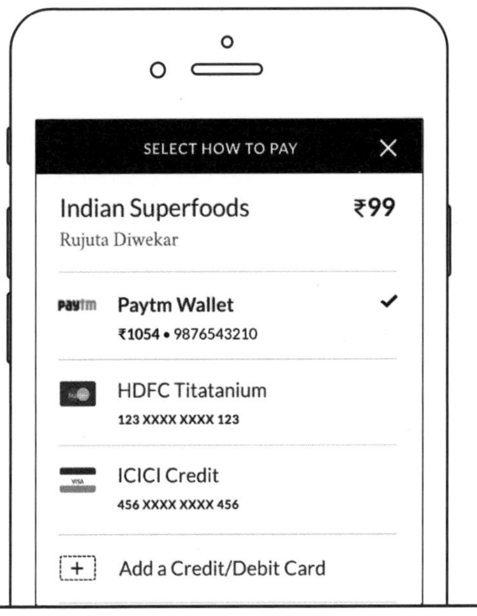

Paytm Wallet, Cards & Apple Payments

On Android, just add a Paytm Wallet once and buy any book with one tap. On iOS, pay with one tap with your iTunes-linked debit/credit card.

Click the QR Code with a QR scanner app or type the link into the Internet browser on your phone to download the app.

SCAN TO READ THIS BOOK ON YOUR PHONE

www.juggernaut.in

DOWNLOAD THE APP

www.juggernaut.in

For our complete catalogue, visit www.juggernaut.in
To submit your book, send a synopsis and two sample chapters to books@juggernaut.in
For all other queries, write to contact@juggernaut.in